STO

FRIENDS
OF ACPL

DI190978

Benjamin Banneker
Genius of Early America

Benjamin Banneker
Genius of Early America

Lillie Patterson

Illustrated by
David Scott Brown

Abingdon   Nashville

Benjamin Banneker, Genius of Early America

Copyright © 1978 by Lillie Patterson

All Rights Reserved

Library of Congress Cataloging in Publication Data

PATTERSON, LILLIE.
  Benjamin Banneker, genius of early America.
  Bibliography: p.
  SUMMARY: A biography of the distinguished
eighteenth-century black astronomer, farmer, mathematician, and surveyor whose accomplishments include having
published a popular almanac and contructed the first
completely American made clock.
  1. Banneker, Benjamin, 19731-1806. 2. Astronomers—
United States—Biography. [1. Banneker, Benjamin, 1731-
1806. 2. Astronomers. 3. Afro-Americans—Biography] I.
Brown, David Scott. II. Title.
QB36.B22P38   520'.92'4 [B] [92]   77-13216
                    ISBN 0-687-02900-7

book designer: Laura Wooten

MANUFACTURED BY THE PARTHENON PRESS AT
NASHVILLE, TENNESSEE, UNITED STATES OF AMERICA

Dedication

A tribute to the black Americans,
known and unknown, whose toil
and genius helped to build and enrich
the United States of America

CO. SCHOOLS
C864236

Acknowledgments

The author wishes to give high praise and thanks to Silvio A. Bedini for the years of research undertaken to complete *The Life of Benjamin Banneker* (Charles Scribner's Sons, 1972). The exhaustive bibliography, documents, and reference notes included in that volume will prove invaluable and timesaving for readers or writers interested in Banneker's life or the period in which he lived.

Special thanks are also due the librarians of the Enoch Pratt Free Library and the Maryland Historical Society for assistance in locating authoritative material on the life of Benjamin Banneker.

Contents

Benjamin Banneker
Genius of Early America

1.   A Story at Bannaky Springs

"Tell me that story again. Please!"

"What story, Benjamin?"

"You know the one I mean. Tell me about how you came across the big ocean on a ship. Tell me how you came to this place."

The woman and her young grandson sat on a bench under a poplar tree in front of their log house. The woman's fair skin had been weathered by wind and sun, and her blond hair was streaked with gray. The boy's dark tan skin was smooth, his black hair a mass of silky curls. The grandmother was white. Her grandson was black. This was part of the story he wanted to hear.

The grandmother sat silent for a moment, her head resting against the tree trunk. Her blue eyes swept the land that stretched downward toward the creek. All around them trees and bushes showed signs of shedding their winter browns for shoots of varied greens. In the cool of the afternoon, an oriole warbled a song of hope. It was springtime in Maryland, 1737.

"Tell me the story," the boy begged again, his large brown eyes alert with curiosity.

The grandmother put a finger under the boy's pointed chin and kissed his nose. "Benjamin Banneker, you are one big question mark," she teased him. "What—when—where—why—how?" Her voice softened. "Very well, I'll tell you again how I came to America.

"I was born in Wessex County, England. My name was Molly Welsh then." Folding her work-roughened hands, the grandmother went on with the story that would be told and written for hundreds of years to come.

Molly Welsh told her grandson how her mother and father had died when she was still a baby. As a young girl, she hired herself out to a dairy farmer. Early every morning she had to go to the barn and help milk the cows. Like many other poor people in the seventeenth century, she worked long hours to earn just enough to pay for her food, clothes, and a place to sleep.

One morning, when Molly was fourteen, something happened that completely changed her life. She got up extra early and began to work fast, filling pail after pail with foaming milk. Suddenly the cow gave a kick. Over went a pail full of milk!

The poor girl knew that she would be punished. She tried to explain the accident to the owner of the dairy farm, but he refused to believe her.

14

The dairyman angrily accused Molly of stealing the milk. Reports had come to him that some of his workers were stealing milk to sell to kitchens on nearby farms. This time, he decided, he would teach all of them a lesson.

He did just that. The dairyman took Molly to court and charged her with stealing. In those days, there were harsh laws that gave poor people severe punishment for stealing food from the rich. Molly might have been put to death. Instead, she was sentenced to be shipped to the English colonies in America to serve seven years of bondage.

So Molly became a "Kings Prisoner," a "Seven-Years Passenger." Hundreds of such prisoners were coming to the colonies during the seventeenth century. This was a way of bringing much-needed workers to the newly settled lands. Any businessman or landowner could sign a contract, called an indenture, to pay for a prisoner's passage. In return, the prisoner worked free for this "master" for a number of years, usually seven.

Interestingly enough, many poor Englishmen who were not prisoners came to the colonies as indentured servants. They came hoping for better opportunities in the New World.

Molly Welsh was fortunate. The ship that brought her in the early 1680s stopped in the colony of Maryland. There her indenture was bought by a rich tobacco farmer who owned a plantation on the Patapsco River.

During the seven years that she served her bondage, the English girl learned all she could about her new homeland. She discovered that poor people, even servants, had the chance to one day own land and become well off. Molly mastered the art of growing tobacco, from seed planting to selling. In the Maryland colony, tobacco was the most important crop, so important that it could be used as currency. People used tobacco receipts to buy goods, to pay debts, and to get credit.

Molly Welsh began dreaming and planning. She worked at extra jobs in her spare time to earn a little money. By the time her years of bondage had ended, she was twenty-two years old. Along with her freedom, the tobacco farmer gave her some money, a few tools, and a cow. With these, the young woman set out to make her way in America. She was tiny and thin, scarcely five feet tall. But she had grown tough and strong, with daring to match the hardy land she now called home.

Much of Maryland was still wilderness. Land was cheap, and there was plenty for anyone willing to clear and develop a tract. Molly took her time, looking, looking for a spot she liked.

She followed the mighty river known to Indians by the lovely name Patapsco, meaning "at the rocky corner." At last she found a place where the river became narrow and branched into two springs. This was the spot. She knew it at once. Here in the fertile hills of the Patapsco River valley, she bought a few acres. She managed to clear enough land to plant a garden and a crop of tobacco in the midst of the trees.

Molly Welsh needed someone to help her cut down the tall timber. She knew of another way of bringing workers into the colonies. Ships sailed from America to Africa and back again, bringing black people who had been captured from their tribal kingdoms. Unlike the indentured servants, the African captives were sold into slavery for life.

Molly decided to use her tobacco and buy a slave or two. She did not like the idea of slavery and promised herself that she would soon free any slaves she bought.

One day in late fall, she went to meet a slave ship that sailed into Chesapeake Bay. The price of slaves was cheaper when bought from a slave ship than from a slave market. The price was cheapest in the fall, when harvesttime was over.

Molly Welsh bought two strong men. The youngest was Bannka, or Bannaka, the captured son of a tribal king in Senegal, Africa. Bannka,

17

who became known as Bannaky, or Banneky, was proud and handsome. He walked with regal steps and held his head high—always acting like the prince he was.

Molly treated her two slaves like members of her family. For the next few years, they helped her clear land, plant fields of corn and tobacco, and build a log house and a tobacco shed. After this was done, she gave them their freedom.

By this time, Molly had fallen in love with the proud African prince. She was impressed by his quiet, thoughtful ways and his keen intelligence. She married Bannaky and took his name. It was not unusual for black slaves and white indentured servants to marry in early America, though new laws were soon passed to forbid this.

Each year Molly and Bannaky raised tobacco and purchased a few more acres of land. Their well-kept farm became one of the best in the Patapsco Valley. The clear springs that flowed from the river, and the Bannaky farm itself, came to be known as Bannaky Springs.

As years went by, the family at Bannaky Springs grew larger. A daughter was born and was given the name Mary. Then three other girls were born to the happy couple.

While the children were still small, Bannaky

died suddenly. This left Molly to run the farm and bring up the children by herself.

The oldest daughter, Mary, became better known than any of her sisters. This, too, is part of the fascinating story of Bannaky Springs. Mary grew up and married a young man who had been captured in Guinea, Africa, and sold as a slave in Maryland. He gained his freedom, became a Christian, and took the first name Robert. Slaves seldom had a last name, and they had no legal rights. Sometimes they took the surname of their owner, or made up one for themselves. Robert took his wife's family name. Over the years the spelling changed from Bannaky to Banneker.

The first child born to Mary and Robert Banneker was a son. He was Benjamin, the boy who listened to Molly as she told the story of the family. Little Benjamin Banneker seemed to sense that his grandmother, her story, the farm, were all part of his heritage in a beautiful land.

2. The Little Landowner

Young Benjamin Banneker opened his eyes before the rooster crowed. The day was going to be exciting. He could feel it, all the way down to his toes.

"Hurry up, day. Start! Hurry up, sun. Shine!"

This was the day for him to go on a trip, a trip all the way to the town of Joppa. In all his six years, he had never been far from the area around Bannaky Springs.

Benjamin could hear his mother moving about, cooking breakfast. The one-story log house was divided into one part for sleeping and the other for cooking and eating. Benjamin slept up in the loft.

Sliding from his bed, he dressed quickly and joined his mother. He stood watching her for a minute as she bent over an iron pot that hung in the wide fireplace. Mary Banneker was beautiful! She was tall and slender, with high cheekbones, and skin the color of light copper. Her heavy black hair hung in two thick braids almost to her waist. Benjamin knew that strangers often mistook his mother for an Indian.

"Good morning, son," she said as she turned

and saw him. "Wash your face and hands. Breakfast will soon be ready."

"I'll put the dishes on the table," Benjamin said quickly. As he set out the tin plates and poured milk into thick mugs, his father came in from the farm.

Robert Banneker was tall and powerful, sturdy as the hickory trees that grew in the woods behind their house. Like the trees, he had pushed down his roots firmly in the Maryland soil. Year after year, he had helped Molly raise tobacco. With his share of the money, he bought a twenty-five-acre tract of woodland next to her farm, a tract called Timber Point.

"Time for breakfast," Benjamin sang out to his father. "Are you ready for the trip?"

Robert Banneker smiled and gave his son a playful hug. "We can leave as soon as we finish eating."

"Then hurry and—" Benjamin stopped and turned with a cry of joy as his grandmother walked through the door. "Hi, Grandma Molly. Are you ready?"

"Ready," she answered, with a kiss. "I've worked and waited a long time for this day."

Benjamin turned to his mother. "Can you come?"

"No, child," she said. "I must stay here with

your three little sisters. They are much too young for the long trip."

The family sat around the wooden table to eat. The food was plentiful and good—boiled hominy, smoked ham, cornbread, and creamy milk. Everything had been raised on their farm. As the Bannekers ate, their faces reflected the joy that overflowed their log house that morning.

Their big dream was about to be realized. This was the day to buy a bigger farm. They had no money, but they had tobacco, and in the colony of Maryland, tobacco was as good as gold.

Season after season, the family at Bannaky Springs had worked together to build their

dream. Even little Benjamin helped. In early spring he went with his father to plant the tiny tobacco seeds—seeds so tiny they looked like ground pepper. In early summer he trudged beside his father, transplanting the tender tobacco shoots from the seedbeds to long rows. As the plants grew, Benjamin went up and down the rows with his mother and grandmother, pulling up weeds from around the roots. Patiently, they picked the tobacco-eating insects from the branching leaves. Finally, in the fall, Benjamin watched as the long, broad leaves were hung in the tobacco shed to be cured.

Now the cured tobacco leaves had been

packed into barrels taller than Benjamin. These were called hogsheads. In each hogshead the leaves were packed tightly around a pole that ran through the center. In this way, the pole acted as an axle, so that the hogshead could be rolled over and over along the road. Many of the Maryland roads had been cut by farmers in order to roll their hogsheads to markets. Some of these "rolling roads" later developed into important highways.

By the time the sun rose above the Patapsco hills, the Bannekers were rolling their hogsheads along the dew-covered road. Robert Banneker used one horse and two oxen to pull the hogsheads along. A second horse pulled the small farm wagon in which Molly and Benjamin rode. As the wagon creaked along, the two riders spent the hours laughing and talking together.

"I talk with you the way I used to talk with your grandfather," Molly told Benjamin. "Sometimes I forget that you are so young." She stayed quiet for a time, a faraway look in her eyes. "You are very much like him, you know," she reminded her grandson. "You have his questioning mind, always wanting to learn something new."

"Tell me some stories about him," Benjamin asked. He never knew Bannaky, who died before his grandson was born. But Molly had talked about the African prince so much that Benjamin could picture him clearly.

On the road to Joppa that morning, Molly told how she and her husband had tamed the wooded land and changed it into a fertile farm. "What a hunter that Bannaky was!" she remembered. "He had learned to hunt in Africa, and could track wild game as well as any Indian."

"Did he learn to like living in this country?" Benjamin wanted to know.

"Yes, he did," Molly said firmly. "Your grandfather had two big dreams. For one thing, he longed for his family to own large tracts of land. For another, he wanted his children and their children to be free and never know slavery. He knew that black people who own land have a higher standing in the eyes of the law and a better chance of staying free."

The boy and his grandmother talked, told stories, and sang throughout the tiresome trip to Joppa. At last they entered the busy river port on the Gunpowder River. People from miles around came to Joppa to buy and sell tobacco.

Benjamin's eyes fairly danced with excitement as he watched the hustle and bustle of the busy port. Molly pointed out the beautiful homes and the towering tobacco warehouses. As they came near the wharf, she told him about the seagoing ships that stood at anchor. "These are English ships," she said. "They are waiting to take tobacco back to England. Ships come here loaded with goods that the colonies cannot yet produce. They return to England loaded with products that we can send to Europe."

"What is that?" Benjamin asked, pointing to a flat-bottomed boat.

"That is a scow, and the boat beside it is a three-masted schooner. They will carry fish and building materials to other American colonies."

Benjamin sniffed the air. "What is that smell—the sweet smell?"

"That is perfume. Rich ladies order perfume to use when they dress up."

"And those big barrels—what's in them?"

"Some are filled with oil, some are filled with molasses."

"Why—" Benjamin's questions came faster than his grandmother could answer them. They stopped when his father rolled his shipment of tobacco into the warehouse to be weighed. Merchants eagerly waited to buy it. In return for the tobacco, a merchant gave tobacco notes, or receipts.

Robert Banneker added these notes to the ones he already held. One by one he counted them, while Molly and Benjamin looked on.

"We have it!" Benjamin's father cried out in

triumph. "We have notes for seven thousand pounds of tobacco, enough to buy the land."

Hand in hand, they walked to the courthouse. In one of the large rooms, a clerk picked up a quill pen and began to write on a long paper.

"The clerk is making out a deed of ownership for the land we will buy," Molly whispered to Benjamin. "A man named Richard Gist is selling the land to us."

"Who is Richard Gist?" Benjamin whispered back.

"A very important person, Benjamin. Richard Gist is one of the men who founded the new Baltimore Town, only ten miles from our home."

"Will you take me to Baltimore Town one day?"

"I hope so, son. You and the new town are about the same age. You were born November 9, 1731. Baltimore was founded in December, 1729." She smiled. "Today, Baltimore is only a settlement, with a wooden fence around it for protection against Indian raids. Someday, it will grow into a great port, far greater than Joppa."

The clerk looked up. "The papers are ready," he said, and began reading aloud from the deed. In return for the price of seven thousand pounds of tobacco, Richard Gist was turning over ownership of a tract of land. Benjamin's heart beat fast when he heard his name, and the

Bannaky family name, read in the Joppa court-house: "The said Robert Bannaky and Benjamin Bannaky, his son, their heirs and assigns forever . . . one hundred acres of land."

Robert Banneker gave the clerk the tobacco notes and took the deed. "The land will be in both our names," he said, putting his arms around his son. "If I should die, it will become yours, for you are the one to carry on the family name."

Benjamin opened his mouth wide, but no sound came out. He, Benjamin Banneker, age six, was a landowner in the Crown Colony of Maryland. For once in his life, the boy was too overcome with excitement to ask a question.

3.   Growing and Learning

It was time for the spring planting. Benjamin moved beside his father, step for step. Up one long row, then down another, they planted corn seeds in the newly turned earth. A part of their new hundred-acre tract had been hastily cleared to make room for larger fields of corn and tobacco.

"Soon as planting is over, I'm going to start building the new house." Robert Banneker's words were measured to match his movements.

"Oh, can I help you?" Benjamin begged. "Please!"

His father laughed. "Of course you can help. I'll teach you how to do everything on this farm. You may have to run the place by yourself one day."

All that summer and fall the Banneker family worked hard with the farming and harvesting. After that they joined together in the exciting venture of building a new house. There was plenty of stout timber on the tract they had bought. In fact, their land was part of a larger tract known as Stout.

After his father had put up the walls of the house, Benjamin helped to chink the spaces between the great logs with clay, first on one side, then on the other. "Why are we doing this?" he wanted to know.

"The clay keeps out the cold wind in winter," his father explained. "It also keeps out the hot sun in summer."

Benjamin even showed his little sisters how they could help with the house. The three pretty girls were strong and healthy. Minta and Molly were the younger two; the name of the oldest sister has been lost to history. They adored their older brother. Running and laughing, they picked up the small pieces of lumber and chips that fell as their father chopped and sawed.

The little girls followed Benjamin into the rocky hills when it was time to gather stones. They picked up the smallest stones, Benjamin carried the medium-sized ones, and their father lugged the largest stones of all. Stone upon stone, Robert Banneker built a chimney, and then he built a fireplace that took up almost one side of the house.

The house was built with a loft, which gave extra space for sleeping and for storage. There were openings for windows, but the family could not yet afford to buy glass panes. They had to settle for heavy wooden shutters. By the time winter set in, the last roof beam was put in place. The family could move their belongings to the snug house.

Benjamin's father spent the winter months making beds and tables from slabs of wood. He had no nails to work with, but he skillfully put the furniture together with wooden pegs. Molly and Mary Banneker made soft mattresses from the feathers they had saved from chickens and geese. As a surprise for the children, their father made each of them a little stool to sit on.

Early the next spring, Benjamin helped his father set out an orchard behind the house—apple, pear, peach, and cherry trees. One afternoon, Robert Banneker came home and began building something at the edge of the orchard.

"What are you making now?" Benjamin questioned.

"A beehive," his father answered. "Come, I'll show you how it's done."

"Honey!" Benjamin called out, running closer to help. "Now we can have honey with our corn cakes." In the middle 1700s, many children in America seldom tasted sweets. Honey was a real treat.

That summer held still another unexpected treat for Benjamin. One day he whistled as he walked up the hill to his grandmother's house. It was the time of day he liked best. Farm chores for the day were done. The late afternoon sun hung lazily over the hills as though reluctant to go down. Leaves were still, fields lay quiet. Everything seemed to be resting at the end of a hot summer day.

Molly Banneker waited for him in the doorway. "I thought you would be here soon." Her blue eyes twinkled. "A surprise is waiting on the table."

"Did you cook something good to eat?" Benjamin asked.

"No, dear. It is something better than food."

Benjamin's wide-set eyes opened and closed playfully, teasing his grandmother. "I give up. Show me the surprise."

"Keep your eyes closed and follow me." Taking his hand, his grandmother led him to a wooden table. Gently, she placed his hands on a large package. "Now, open your eyes."

"What's inside?" Benjamin grew more excited by the minute.

Together, they untied the heavy package. As the last bit of wrapping fell away, the boy gave a gasp of surprise. "A book! A big, big book."

"The Great Book," Molly said in a low voice. "This is the Holy Bible."

"Where did it come from? Joppa? Baltimore Town?"

"Benjamin, Benjamin, this Bible came all the way from England. I ordered it so that we could read it together."

"But I can't read—"

"You will learn to read soon. This Bible will teach you." Slowly, Molly guided Benjamin's finger over the opening lines of the first chapter: "In the beginning . . ."

That moment was indeed a beginning for Benjamin Banneker. His lessons in reading started that very day. His grandmother had taught him the ABC's earlier, so reading came easily. On some days, Molly helped him to learn the words for himself. On other days, she read aloud the thrilling stories of the saints and heroes.

The Bible became Benjamin's textbook. There were few schools, or even books, in Maryland and the other colonies at this time. Books were costly. Rich families usually hired private tutors for their children. The children of poor families were taught to read and count by their parents—if their parents knew how. Children of black families, even free black families, had little chance for formal book learning.

Benjamin's grandmother inspired him with a guide for self-teaching. "Learning is an adventure. Wherever you are, at any age, there is something new to find out."

33

As Benjamin grew older, his eager mind discovered the many ways of learning from the world about him. History and geography came alive through songs and storytelling. From his grandmother he found out facts about English history and heard stories and songs that described English country life. From his father he learned about the glorious kings and kingdoms of West Africa. He listened to tales of tribal life and clapped to the rhythmic African songs and dances.

As he began to explore the outdoor world, Benjamin learned other facts. He went fishing with his father and soon knew in which season to catch the catfish, rockfish, shad, sheepshead, and eel, all fishes that swam in nearby waters. His father taught him to hunt and trap. The ducks, deer, turkeys, rabbits, and other animals furnished plenty of meat for their tables. Wolves, panthers, and wildcats still roamed the wilderness not far from their farm. Though Benjamin was not old enough to hunt large animals, he watched as his father tanned the pelts that were used for clothing in cold weather.

With no other boy near enough to have as a playmate, Benjamin learned to spend his hours alone. He took long walks through the quiet woods, studying the trees—the chestnuts, oaks, maples, hickories, poplars, and beeches. At an early age he learned to observe things closely and to remember details of what he saw. The sky and ground and all between became for him an inexhaustible schoolhouse.

By the time Benjamin was eleven years old, however, his mind reached far beyond the familiar woods and streams. He wanted books. He longed to go school, to study with other scholars. There was so much he wanted to know, more than his grandmother and his parents could tell him.

What would happen to him as he grew older? He often pondered the question—what next?

CO. SCHOOLS

C864236

4. A School at Last

Benjamin and his grandmother worked together, topping tobacco plants. Holding each green shoot, they carefully cut off the topmost part. This caused the remaining leaves to grow large and lush as the plant developed.

"And why are you so quiet this morning?" Benjamin frowned as he asked the question.

Molly took a long time to answer. "I am quiet because I have a lot on my mind. Another stranger has moved into the next valley."

"Who is he?" As usual, Benjamin fired one question after another. "Is he a farmer? Why did he come?"

"I have heard that he is a Quaker."

"A Quaker? What does that mean?"

"It means, Benjamin, that he belongs to a religious group called the Society of Friends."

"But why do you call him a Quaker?"

Knowing that Benjamin's curiosity must be satisfied, his grandmother talked to him about Quakerism. She knew about it because the Quaker movement had started in England. She told about George Fox, the devout Englishman who had organized the Friends. "They believe in plainness of dress and belongings and in friendliness and goodwill," Molly Banneker recalled.

"But where did this Quaker come from?" Benjamin asked.

"Your father told me that he comes from Pennsylvania. I know there are many Quakers there in the colony settled by the Friends, who came to America about the time I did."

Benjamin still had more questions. "But why did this Quaker come here?"

"He has already planted a farm." Molly topped three more plants before she said the next words. "I also heard that he is well educated and plans to open a school in the fall."

"A school!" Benjamin jumped across his row and stood in front of his grandmother. "A real school?"

Molly smoothed her long white apron. "I'll try to find out all I can about it, son. I know that Quakers have started small schools in many places, and they take in poor children free of charge. If there is a school, you will be a pupil. I will see to that."

The news proved to be true. The Quaker farmer planned to open his school as soon as the crops were harvested. Benjamin's father and grandmother lost no time in going to visit the schoolmaster, who agreed to take the boy as one of the students.

"My school will be open to all children," the schoolmaster told them. "Send the lad to me."

A school! Benjamin talked about it every day that summer. "Will the Quaker teacher like me?" he wondered aloud to his grandmother.

"He will, child." Off and on that summer Benjamin's grandmother told him more about the Quakers. "The Friends believe in equality of all people regardless of their race or religion or where they come from. They were the first group in the world to speak out against slavery."

By summer's end, Benjamin was as curious about the teacher as he was about the school. He helped with the harvest, knowing that teachers did not open their schools until after the hard farm work was done.

Finally, the big day came. Early that morning, Benjamin dressed in a new homespun suit. His mother had spun the cloth, and his grandmother had made the coat and pants. Waving good-bye to his family, he ran along the trail that led to the Quaker's farm. "New suit, new season, new school," he sang as he walked briskly along. "New, new, new!" Benjamin Banneker was off to a new adventure.

When he came to the farm, he found out that

there was no school building—not yet. The teacher held classes in a small room of his house.

"Come in, lad," the schoolmaster greeted Benjamin. "I have looked forward to meeting thee. Welcome!"

Three children had already arrived. In a short time, others came to join them. Benjamin noticed that two of the other pupils had dark skin like his own.

The schoolmaster's quiet, friendly manner put the new students at ease. Benjamin listened in fascination to the way the teacher talked. Instead of using *you* and *your*, the Quaker used *thee* and *thy* and *thou*.

"Here is thy hornbook," the schoolmaster said to Benjamin, handing him a strange-looking small board. "Study it well."

Benjamin held the hornbook carefully in his hands. The "book" was really a flat piece of board with a handle, shaped like a paddle. On the board was pasted a sheet of paper, with simple lessons for beginning pupils. Since paper was scarce and costly, the board was covered with a thin piece of clear horn to protect the lessons.

To Benjamin's delight, he found that he could read everything printed on his hornbook. He quickly named the letters of the alphabet. Next he counted the numbers printed on the hornbook. Last of all he read the Lord's Prayer, which his grandmother had taught him from the Bible.

The teacher came to hear him read. "Well done, Master Benjamin," he praised. "Tomorrow I will let thee study with the older scholars."

That night Benjamin's face lit up bright as the autumn fire as he told his family about his first day at school. He even tried to imitate the speech pattern of his teacher, using *thee* and *thy*.

His grandmother nodded in understanding. "I forgot to tell you about the way many Quakers speak. Would you like to know how this custom started?"

In England, Molly Banneker explained, it was once the custom to use *thee* when addressing someone thought to be a social inferior and *you* for a superior. Common people were told to address their betters as *you* and to remove their hats. Because of their belief in the equality of all persons, Quakers refused to do either. They decided to us *thee* and *thou* for any person, regardless of social position.

The next morning, Benjamin went to school with even greater admiration for his teacher. On that day, and the days that followed, he was one of the first students to arrive and the last to leave.

One of the black students, Jacob Hall, soon became Benjamin's best friend. The black students were all children of free parents. Jacob wanted fun and games in his spare time, but not Benjamin. "All his delight was to dive into his books," Jacob Hall later remembered about his friend.

The only book Benjamin's family owned was his grandmother's Bible. After a few weeks, the kind schoolmaster began lending the eager student some of the books from his small library—texts on literature, history, and mathematics.

Everyone in the Banneker family shared Benjamin's joy in going to school. During long winter evenings, while they roasted chestnuts in the fireplace, the boy played school with his sisters. By the light of bayberry candles made by his mother, he taught them to read and write, to spell and count. And every night before the family went to bed, he read aloud from the Bible, the beautiful language lilting softly through the log cabin.

The Quaker teacher and the school opened up a new world for young Benjamin Banneker. Each day he discovered new continents of learning to explore. Soon he was studying mathematics with the best scholars in the school. For Benjamin, working with numbers was like working with a never-ending puzzle. There were always parts to be added, divided, made larger or smaller, taken

BENJAMIN BANNEKER

apart, and put together again.

The schooling stopped each year when seed-time came. Like Benjamin, most of the students were needed to help on farms. In the fall, when harvest ended, the school reopened.

So the years passed, with Benjamin growing taller with each school term. As he grew older, he became more serious. While other scholars romped in the schoolyard, he sat indoors and read. Many days he would linger after the other children had gone home, questioning the teacher about facts that had caught his fancy.

By the time Benjamin was fifteen, his schooling had to stop. His father's health began to fail, and the boy was needed on the farm all year round. Besides, as the teacher explained, Benjamin had learned just about everything he could in the one-room school. He knew enough now to study on his own.

"I will continue to lend thee my books," the Quaker teacher promised.

"Thank you." Benjamin grasped his teacher's hand. "I will keep on studying," he promised in return.

He kept his word. There were so many things a person could teach himself, he discovered. Benjamin Banneker's great adventure in learning had only begun.

42

5. The Wonderful Wooden Clock

Benjamin Banneker celebrated his twentieth birthday in 1751. He had grown tall and strong. He walked the way his Grandfather Bannaky used to walk, his shoulders squared, his head held high. He was handsome like his grandfather, with a broad forehead, wide-spaced, dreamy eyes, and pointed chin.

Benjamin needed his strength, for much of the farm work now fell to him. The years of toil had weakened his grandmother's thin frame. One day she lay down peacefully and never woke again. She had lived to see her beloved grandson grow to manhood and receive a basic education. He would carry on the farming and the family name, she knew.

Benjamin's father could no longer work hard, as his health grew poorer day by day. The oldest girl in the family had married and was now Mrs. Henden, living in a distant community. The younger girls, Minta and Molly, helped out as best they could. Their mother did the cooking and the gardening. It was Benjamin, however, who shouldered most of the farming responsibilities.

Hard work did not stop his studying. While he plowed and planted, hoed and harvested, his mind was on the interesting bits and pieces of information he was learning. How he missed his grandmother! She, more than anyone else in the family, had understood his mind. He missed the long talks they would have together.

To fill the void left by his grandmother's death, Benjamin concentrated upon the study of mathematics. He especially liked algebra and geometry, for they challenged his thinking. As he got to know the neighboring farmers, he used his skill with numbers to help them. Many of these farmers had never been to school and could not read or write. Benjamin showed them how to weigh their tobacco properly, and he assisted them in figuring the value of their tobacco receipts.

He would meet these farmers when he went to the river landings to sell or trade tobacco from his own farm. One morning he got up unusually early and dressed in his best clothes. Because of his friendship and admiration for his Quaker teacher, he adopted many of the Quaker customs and ways of thinking. He usually wore a long, plain coat and a broadbrimmed hat, the familiar dress of Quaker men.

"I am off to Elk Ridge Landing," Benjamin

told his mother. "Many tobacco merchants will be coming there today." He mounted his favorite horse and rode away.

At the landing, he met a merchant with whom he liked to trade. As the two talked, the merchant suddenly took something from his pocket.

Benjamin stared at the object, his eyes wide with interest. "May I see that?" he asked, forgetting all about the business at hand.

"Of course you may see my pocket watch." The merchant held the timepiece on his palm. "I ordered it from England last year," he said. "Have you never seen a watch before?"

"Never!" Benjamin bent his head to look closer. "I have seen a sundial, but never a clock or a watch. May I hold it for a moment?"

The watch in Benjamin's hand seemed almost alive, ticking as though it breathed. He watched the tiny hands move slowly around and around, marking off the minutes. Holding the pocket watch to his ear, he listened to the regular rhythm of its movements.

A new adventure in learning was about to begin. The thought of the watch made Benjamin dizzy with excitement. He knew that many rich people in the colonies owned clocks and watches, but they lived in cities. He knew of no clock in the rural area where he lived. Yet he was holding a real timepiece in his hand.

The kind merchant was struck by the black man's interest in his watch. "Would you like to borrow it for a few weeks?" he asked. "You could return it when you come to sell me your tobacco."

"Yes, yes, thank you," Benjamin answered. "I will treasure it like a jewel."

He rode home, his mind whirling with new ideas. As he moved along, he measured his horse's gait to the tick-ticking in his pocket.

Minta and Molly met him, astonished to see the treasure their brother had brought. That night the family watched while Benjamin put the watch on a table and began to study it. A few nights later, they stared in disbelief as he picked up a small knife. Working ever so carefully, he began to pry the back from the watch.

The two sisters leaned over Benjamin's shoulders, scarcely breathing. "You're not going to take it apart?" Molly asked.

"How else will I discover how it works?" he retorted, never taking his eyes from the watch.

"Can you put the pieces back together?" Minta worried.

Benjamin grinned. "Anything I can take apart, I can put together again."

Every night that week he sat studying the inner workings of the timepiece. He marveled at the tiny gears and wheels, observing the way they moved. Working like an artist, he drew each part—the wheels, the gears, the springs. By the time he returned the watch to the merchant several weeks later, his drawings were finished. He had memorized every detail of the watch, inside and outside.

"What now?" Benjamin's father asked him.

"It's time for me to do some figuring," Benjamin decided. "I know enough mathematics to figure out plans for the clock I will make."

"A clock?" The family looked at Benjamin as though he had lost his mind.

"What will you use?" his mother wanted to know.

Benjamin never blinked an eye. "I will use what I have."

What he had, and plenty of it, was wood. He picked out pieces of hard-grained wood and seasoned them well. After the harvest was over that year, he began to whittle away at the wood.

During the winter days, when fields lay resting under frost or snow and the fire roared in the chimney, Benjamin cut and whittled the pieces of wood. His knowledge of mathematics served him well. Careful mathematical calculations had to be made in order to determine the size of each part of the clock he planned.

Every part had to be precisely cut and measured. First Benjamin carved the teeth of the wheelwork. This alone took months. Time after time he made the wheels, only to find that the parts did not fit together properly. Patiently, he would put the old parts aside and start to make new ones.

Spring returned, and it was planting time. Benjamin worked in the fields by day and labored over his clock at night. Sometimes the parts proved too big, sometimes they were too small. "This is much like a puzzle," Benjamin told his family. "I never give up on any puzzle until I have solved it."

Finally the day came when all the parts were finished. With a sigh of relief, Benjamin began to put them together.

"Oh, no!" His groan of disappointment told the story. The hour and the minute hands moved, but they did not move in a way to tell perfect time. No matter how well Benjamin had made each separate part, he knew that all parts had to work as a unit. Only then could his clock tell time correctly.

The amateur clockmaker refused to give up. Over and over he used his calculations—figuring, measuring, cutting, thinking. For well-nigh two years he labored over the clock. At last, late one night, his family heard him give a cry of triumph.

"They fit!" All the parts worked together—as perfectly as the pieces of a neat puzzle. The clock was made entirely of wood except for the striking parts, which had to be made from iron and brass.

At first Benjamin set the clock to strike every hour. Finding that this loud striking kept the family awake at night, he adjusted the workings to strike at six and again at twelve.

Happily, Benjamin made a sturdy case and a dial for his timepiece. Then he hung it on the wall beside the fireplace.

So it was that in 1753, at age twenty-two, Benjamin Banneker made the first striking clock with all parts made entirely in America. Other clocks had been made in the colonies, no doubt, but at least some of the parts had been made in Europe. Most of the colonial clockmakers had been trained in England.

Word of the wonderful wooden clock spread rapidly. People came from miles around to see the marvel.

"Amazing!" some visitors said, gazing at the timepiece. "What expert craftsmanship."

"Unbelievable!" others cried, looking at the

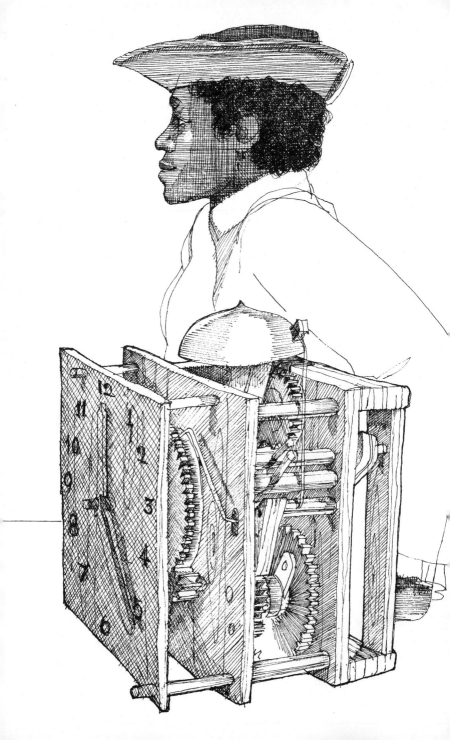

young black man who had made it. "Benjamin Banneker is a genius."

The fame of the clockmaker spread all over the Patapsco Valley and beyond. The clock became one of the wonders of the day. Benjamin, the farmer, became better known as Banneker, the inventor.

6.   Farming and Studying

Benjamin Banneker left his tobacco field to help his mother work in her herb garden. It was late summer, 1762.

Despite her advancing age, Mary Banneker was still a trim, spry woman. Her hair was glossy black, with no hint of gray. She had become known throughout the region for her knowledge of herbs. In her fragrant garden she grew such herbs as snakeroot, ginseng, and sassafras. She also knew how to search the meadows and woodlands for wild plants that could be used to cure illnesses. Since there was no doctor nearby, her neighbors sought her help when they had sickness in their families.

As Banneker and his mother worked together, they talked about changes that had taken place in their family life.

"The farm seems quiet with so many of the family gone," Banneker said quietly.

"Too quiet," his mother agreed. "The two of us must keep things going."

Banneker now found himself head of the household. His younger sisters had married, but both lived on farms within walking distance.

Minta was now Mrs. Black, and Molly was Mrs. Morton. Robert Banneker's health had steadily worsened, and he died in 1759. This left Benjamin and his mother to live in the log house. The two grew closer together as they worked to keep the farm prospering.

As they left the herb garden that day and entered their home, they heard the clock sound the hour of six. Through the seasons, the family had marked their work-time and sleep-time by the striking of the wooden clock.

While his mother prepared their evening meal, Banneker fed his horses, herd of cows, and dozens of chickens. After supper, mother and son sat under a wide-spreading chestnut tree that grew near the house. Together they watched the sunset spread a splendor over the Patapsco hills.

Mary Banneker worked on a broom she was making from reeds gathered from the river-banks. Benjamin Banneker began to play his violin. As he drew the bow across the strings, the music rose and fell, sometimes sad, some-times gay. Whenever his mother heard a melody she knew, she hummed the tune softly.

After a time, the music maker put aside the violin and played a flute. During his years of self-study, he had taught himself music. The flute and the violin were his favorite instruments.

The music suddenly stopped. Boom! Still and tense, Banneker and his mother sat listening. Boom! Boom! Boom! The roar of a cannon shook the silence.

"The sound comes from the plantation of Mr. William Williams, the rich merchant," Banneker said. "He has a cannon mounted on a lofty hill."

"You know what it means, don't you?" It was more a statement than a question from his mother.

"Yes. A cannon in the morning calls all slaves to work. When a cannon booms at sunset, it sends a message." Benjamin explained the message to his mother. Several times a year, he reminded her, rich plantation owners imported large stocks of goods from England. They always bought more than they needed and sold the extra goods to small farmers of the region. A cannon was fired at sunset to let these farmers know when a new shipment arrived.

"Will you be going to buy something?" Mary Banneker asked.

"First thing in the morning," Benjamin answered quickly. "Mr. Williams loves the violin, and he may have ordered a few extra sheets of music." He gave his mother a teasing smile. "If there is something pretty, I may bring it back for you."

Before sunup next day he was on his way. He rode one of his two horses and led the other one to use as a packhorse for his purchases. Following along old Indian trails, he reached a rolling road. This led to the huge plantation of the rich importer.

Other farmers were already gathered there. Slaves hurried back and forth, putting the goods out on tables or spreading them on the spacious lawn. Each farmer began choosing the things he could afford.

Banneker picked out some farm tools and supplies—a rake, a plow, a knife, two hoes. Moving to another table, he bought a pair of shoes for himself. On still another table, he found yards of colorful embroidered satin material. He bought enough for his mother to make a fine dress. Last of all, he found a piece of music he longed to own.

His purchases made, Banneker lingered to listen to the other farmers as they talked together. His eager ears picked up every scrap of news as the men exchanged ideas about the weather, government, farming methods, and ways of mending farm tools.

When the group broke up, one of the youngest farmers pulled Banneker aside. "I am starting a new barn next week," the farmer whispered. "Would you be kind enough to help me figure the measurements?"

"Why, of course." Benjamin's manner was courteous.

Another man overheard them. "Lucky I met you today," he told Banneker. "I need to get word to my kinfolk in Virginia. Could you possibly write another letter for me?"

"Glad to, sir." Banneker bowed as he spoke. He knew that these farmers considered him the best-educated person in the region. From the time he started to school, he always welcomed a chance to share his learning with other people. After all, he reasoned, teaching others is one good way of learning more yourself.

Benjamin Banneker made another important purchase early the following year. He bought a large edition of the Holy Bible. The day he bought it, he thought a great deal about his grandmother, and about how her Bible had started him on the road to studying. "I will read part of this book every day of my life," he promised himself.

Reaching for a quill pen, Banneker opened the Bible and wrote on the flyleaf:

I bought this book of Honora Buchanan the 4th day of January, 1763. B.B.

In his large, firm penmanship, Banneker recorded two other important family events in the Bible.

Benjamin Banneker was born November the 9th, in the year of the Lord God, 1731.

Robert Banneker departed this life July the 10th, 1759.

Father—son, Banneker reflected, the past and the present. What would the future hold for him?

He was determined that the future would hold time for study as well as work. He was thirty-two years old, and his mind yearned for face-to-face interchange with other men interested in reading, in mathematics, in world affairs.

This seemed impossible. He was a black man, living in a rather remote section of the country. How could he make this small world larger? How?

The answer came soon—and unexpectedly.

7. The Ellicotts
of Ellicott's Mills

"New neighbors are moving into the Hollow."

The surprising news spread from one farm to another in the Patapsco Valley. "Who are these strangers?" farmers asked each other. "Why are they hacking a road through the rocky wilderness?"

No farmer was more curious than Benjamin Banneker. The bottomland called the Hollow was only a mile from the edge of his farm. One day he stood on a hill to watch the sights for himself. The next day he was back, and the next.

The goings-on in the Hollow grew too interesting for him to miss. Two tall men directed a team of workmen. Banneker noted that the two men wore the familiar, plain, long coat and broad-brimmed hat and guessed that they were Quakers.

The two men led their workers as they hacked away at the tangled vines, bushes, and trees. Bit by bit, they hewed a roadway through the rocky hillside. The nearest and most direct route from the river landing to the Hollow followed a tortuous route up the hillside. The strangers used this direct route to make their road.

After the rough road was finished, the new-comers brought in supplies and equipment by boat as far as Elk Ridge Landing. From there they began to transport these belongings into the Hollow.

Banneker watched in fascination. "Now, what will they do when they come to the steep precipice?" he wondered aloud. "The horses will never pull wagons over that rocky hill."

To his amazement, the strangers began to unload their wagons and carts. Piece by piece, they took the equipment apart, loaded the pieces in large wheelbarrows, and rolled them over the rocky hills. Back and forth they went, carrying tools, millstones, iron shafts, household goods, and other supplies. Last of all they took the wagons apart and carried them in pieces, leading their horses behind them.

"These strangers are daring men," Banneker reported to his mother. "I must get to know them."

Mary Banneker smiled in understanding. "I am only glad that it is winter, with no heavy farmwork to be done. You will probably spend the season watching our new neighbors."

She was right. Banneker decided to do more than watch. He made up his mind to meet the strangers.

As it happened, they came to him. One day

the two men walked up to his farm. "We are your neighbors," one of the men began. "I am John Ellicott, and this is my brother, Andrew."

Banneker was so delighted that he forgot he was with strangers. "I am Benjamin Banneker, and I am proud to know you," he greeted them.

The Ellicott brothers showed their pleasure in the meeting by shaking Banneker's hand firmly. In America of the early 1770s, it was quite uncommon for a white man to call a black man "mister" and shake his hand, no matter how friendly they were. The Ellicotts were Quakers, as Banneker had surmised, and they practiced their belief in the equality of all races.

During their conversation that day, Banneker discovered that the neighbors were moving to Maryland from Bucks County, Pennsylvania. "There are three other brothers," John Ellicott explained. "Joseph will join us soon. Thomas and Nathaniel will remain in Pennsylvania."

"We are here to build a flour mill on the falls of the Patapsco River," Andrew Ellicott added.

"A mill!" Banneker's face showed his surprise. "Is that wise? This is tobacco country." He informed his guests that a few farmers grew wheat for their own use, but none of them grew it for sale.

The Ellicotts were firm in their plans. These

plans included growing acres of wheat on their own farms, they told Banneker. They also hoped to convince farmers that they, too, could grow wheat as well as tobacco for profit.

The spot was perfect for a mill. On this the three men agreed. The many rivers and deep-water ports could provide transportation for the grain and flour. Baltimore Town, scarcely ten miles away, had the fine harbors necessary for developing into a great shipping port.

"Well, I wish you luck, sirs," Banneker said. "Since we are neighbors, perhaps I can be of service to you."

"Perhaps," the Ellicotts agreed. Their big problem was food, especially fresh vegetables.

Banneker flashed his friendly smile. "I will make that my problem, neighbors. My mother and I will help you find what you need."

He kept his word. Each week for the next year, Banneker and his mother saw that fresh eggs, vegetables, fruits, herbs, and honey were taken to the millsite. In addition, Banneker showed the neighbors which streams had the best fish and where to hunt the finest game—and he helped them in countless other ways.

Each time he visited the millsite, Banneker liked the Ellicotts better. They were such brilliant men! All of them shared his interest in reading and in mathematics. All seemed to have mechanical skills. At last Banneker had the face-to-face contact with learned men he wanted. He made the most of it.

Never had he imagined the kinds of machinery that were used in building the great gristmill. He watched day after day as the parts of the giant mill were put together. After a few weeks, he was not only watching but giving suggestions. When the stone mill was finally finished, it towered as tall as a two-story house.

By then the Ellicotts had built temporary living quarters, stables, and a sawmill. At the end of two years, a village community known as Ellicott's Lower Mills was thriving in the Hollow. The section where a second mill was built became Ellicott's Upper Mills.

Benjamin Banneker's friendship with the Ellicott family grew stronger over the next few years. The brothers came often to Banneker's cottage to sit and talk. They were as interested in the farmer and his clock as Banneker was in them and in their mill. After the brothers built their permanent homes, they invited Banneker to come and visit with their families.

Joseph Ellicott built a two-story mansion at Upper Mills. He was a clockmaker, and he delighted in showing Banneker his marvelous collection of timepieces. The prized item was a four-sided clock, made in the form of a pillar, or column, and towering eight feet high. One face showed the sun, moon, and all the planets moving in their orbits. On a second face were the hands that traced the minutes, hours, days, weeks, and months. A third dial showed the names of twenty-four musical tunes that chimed, one for each passing hour. The fourth face was a glass plate through which observers could examine the intricate wheelwork.

Joseph Ellicott explained to Banneker how his son, Andrew IV, had helped him design the unique clock. Andrew was only fifteen when they made it.

What exciting people to have as neighbors! With the coming of the Ellicott family, Banneker's world began to widen considerably.

8. A Young Friend Named George

The member of the Ellicott family who visited Banneker most often was young George. He was the son of Andrew Ellicott, one of the brothers who had built the mills. George was only twelve years old when his family moved to Maryland. He had heard about the remarkable Benjamin Banneker even before he came, and the two became fast friends from their first meeting.

Banneker looked forward to his young friend's visits. George was a likable lad, with an extremely handsome face and a shock of curly hair. The two friends never thought about the difference in their ages because their minds worked so well together. They shared a common interest in mathematics, literature, and anything mechanical.

George Ellicott would bring his books to Banneker's cottage, and the two would study for hours at a time. Sometimes the young man was the teacher. At other times, he became Banneker's pupil. It all depended upon which of them knew most about the subject being studied.

As George grew older, his uncles taught him

the science of surveying. By the time he was sixteen, he had become a skilled surveyor. The surveyors, men who measured land to establish the location, form, or boundaries of a certain tract were very important to the growth of the American colonies. As the various sections of the country were settled, surveyors were needed to fix the boundaries of towns and cities and to lay out roads and highways.

George Ellicott brought his textbooks and surveying instruments to Banneker's home, and the two put their heads together and planned projects. When George, only seventeen, laid out an important roadway from Ellicott's Mills to Baltimore, he talked over the plans with Banneker. And as Banneker learned more about surveying, he practiced on his sprawling farm, marking off boundary lines and mapping roadways.

Meanwhile, the settlement at Ellicott's Mills continued to flourish. The family bought a water lot in Baltimore and built their own wharf. They built a general store, which also housed the post office.

This store–post office soon became the communication hub of the entire region. People came to send and pick up their mail. They stopped to examine the goods the Ellicotts imported from England, brought by ships that took their flour to that country.

The men of the region would linger in the store to exchange news of the day. The Ellicott brothers encouraged Banneker to join these gatherings. At first he would sit quietly and listen while the other men talked. Before long, however, he was taking part in the lively conversations. Because of his extensive reading and his keen memory, he could discuss wide-ranging topics.

One of the clerks in the Ellicott & Co. store later recalled how much he enjoyed Banneker's company: "I was always anxious to wait upon him. After making his purchases, he usually went to the part of the store where George Ellicott was in the habit of sitting, to converse with him about the affairs of our government, and other matters. He was very precise in conversation and exhibited deep reflection. His deportment, whenever I saw him, was perfectly upright and correct, and he seemed to be acquainted with everything of importance that was passing in the country."

Two topics of importance in the mid-1770s were taxes and revolution. The American colonists were then in rebellion against England because of unfair tax and trade laws. They wanted changes.

Through his visits to Ellicott's Mills, Banneker kept up with the fast-moving events. In 1775, colonists and British soldiers clashed at Lexington and Concord. The American Revolution began. In 1776, the colonies declared their independence from England. A new nation—the United States of America—was born.

Benjamin Banneker kept up with the news and worked harder than ever, raising wheat and corn to feed the soldiers. He celebrated with the Ellicotts when peace and victory came in 1783. After that, the young United States began to stretch and grow. George Washington was chosen as the first President. Banneker knew that he and Washington had been born less than a year apart.

Like many of his countrymen, Benjamin Banneker held high hopes for his new nation. He memorized the words of Thomas Jefferson written into the Declaration of Independence: "We hold these truths to be self-evident, that all man are created equal, that they are endowed by their Creator with certain unalienable rights, that among these are life, liberty, and the pursuit of happiness."

Surely, Banneker hoped, these words meant that the black slaves, working to build the nation, would be given liberty and the chance to pursue happiness. Surely the slave system

68

would end. But, as the years passed, he knew this was not to be—not yet. So the future stretched ahead for Benjamin Banneker, as mysterious as one of the mathematical puzzles he loved to create.

These mathematical puzzles provided popular entertainment in the eighteenth century. There were few forms of amusement, so people learned to find relaxation by creating and solving mathematical puzzles. The ability to make up and solve these puzzles was considered a sign of high intelligence. Gentlemen exchanged their games back and forth through letters.

Banneker received many letters asking for some of the puzzles he made up and seeking his help in solving others. His friend, George Ellicott, shared this hobby. The two took delight in trying to stump each other with difficult puzzles.

One day Banneker created one that kept George Ellicott working away for days to come up with the correct answer. Like many of Banneker's puzzles, this one was written in verse form. The characters are a vintner, a person who sells wine, and a cooper, a person who makes and repairs barrels. Coopers were much in demand after the Ellicotts began shipping barrels of flour to Europe.

BENJAMIN BANNEKER

A cooper and vintner sat down for a talk,
Both being so groggy that neither could walk;
Says cooper to vintner, "I'm the first of my trade,
There's no kind of vessel but what I have made,
And of any shape, sir, just what you will,
And of any size, sir, from a tun to a gill."

"Then," says the vintner, "you're the man for me.
Make me a vessel, if we can agree.
The top and the bottom diameter define,
To bear that proportion as fifteen to nine,
Thirty-five inches are just what I crave,
No more and no less in the depth will I have;
Just thirty-nine gallons this vessel must hold,
Then I will reward you with silver or gold,—
Give me your promise, my honest old friend."
"I'll make it tomorrow, that you may depend!"

So, the next day, the cooper, his work to discharge,
Soon made the new vessel, but made it too large;
He took out some staves, which made it too small,
And then cursed the vessel, the vintner, and all.
He beat on his breast, "By the powers" he swore
He never would work at his trade any more.
Now, my worthy friend, find out if you can,
The vessel's dimensions, and comfort the man!

George Ellicott never let on to anyone whether
he was able to unriddle the mathematical prank
without help from Banneker. Many other men
tried to solve the puzzle-poem and met with
failure. One mathematician who worked out the

answer was able to determine the size of the container in Banneker's problem. According to him, the great diameter, the top, is 24.745 inches, and the smaller diameter, the bottom, is 14.8476 inches.

The study of mathematics led Benjamin Banneker and George Ellicott into a new adventure in learning. One day George introduced his friend and neighbor to the world of astronomy. "There is no other branch of science quite like it," George insisted. "Together, friend, we will explore the map of the heavens."

Thirsty for knowledge, Banneker soaked up the challenge. Most of the Ellicott men, he knew, had developed an interest in astronomy. From his uncles and cousins George began to learn the science of the stars and the other heavenly bodies.

"We need more time to study together," Banneker said to his friend in a wistful tone. "I am busy with my farm, and the growing mill business keeps you on the go . . . "

George stopped him. "I'll remedy that soon. I have already ordered some new textbooks from England. They will be the best astronomy texts in the world. When they arrive, we will make more time for study."

Later that night Banneker stood looking at the

sky above his farm. "Ah!" His inquiring mind leaped ahead, exploding with thoughts of studying the world beyond the familiar land and water. "Astronomy," he whispered to the wind that teased the trees on the Patapsco hills. "Astronomy!"

9. Studying the Sky

Banneker worked in the fields all morning, stripping tobacco leaves from their stalks. It was harvesttime, 1788.

Just before noon, farmer Banneker stopped to fix some lunch. As he walked toward the house, he thought again how much he missed his mother. Mary Banneker had died several months before, and Banneker now lived alone. His two sisters Minta and Molly came by weekly to take care of his washing, ironing, and mending. Banneker knew how to cook the simple meals he liked to eat.

As he picked up a pan, the wooden clock struck twelve. A moment later he heard the clop-clop of hoofbeats coming into his yard. "Anyone home?" a man called out.

Banneker knew the familiar voice. "Come in, good friend," he greeted George Ellicott. "Here, let me give you a hand with your load."

Tall, handsome, and smiling, George Ellicott entered the room, his arms loaded with books and two cases. "I meant to bring these long before this, but I've been away," he said, putting the books on a table. "The books finally arrived from England."

Banneker looked from the books to the cases. "Are these for me?" His voice quivered with anticipation.

"Indeed, they are," George answered as he opened the larger case.

"A telescope!" Banneker's expression showed his amazement. "Does this mean that you will lend me your telescope as well as your books?"

"They are all for you to use for as long as you like." George held up one of the books. "Read this one first. It was written for beginning students."

Banneker read the title aloud: *"An Easy Introduction to Astronomy."*

"It is easy," George assured him. "The author, James Ferguson, is one of the foremost astronomers in the world." He grinned. "The book belongs to my friend Elizabeth Brooke. I gave it to her as a gift, hoping she would become as interested in astronomy as I am. She likes you, and she especially wanted you to share the gift."

"So you are still courting the beautiful Elizabeth Brooke!" Banneker teased. "Well, give her my humble regards and thanks. I admire her very much." Banneker had met the young woman George was courting and knew her as the daughter of James Brooke, Sr., a large planter in a nearby section of Maryland. It was James Brooke who had founded the settlement that developed into the town of Sandy Spring.

George Ellicott looked at his pocket watch. "I must hurry. Today I leave for a business trip that will keep me away for a long time. As soon as I get back, I will give you some lessons in using the telescope." His voice dropped to a whisper. "I'll tell you a secret. Next year I hope to build a big house, with a special room for a large telescope."

"I—I—I can never thank you enough." Banneker's voice trembled with emotion.

"Think nothing of it." George Ellicott put a hand on Banneker's shoulder. "You have helped my family in countless ways. It is my pleasure to do something for you in return."

The two friends walked to the doorway and stood talking for a few minutes, recalling how the mills had grown.

"You have convinced farmers that wheat is a profitable crop for them," Banneker mentioned.

"Positively," George agreed. "The flour mills are thriving more each day—so much so that they keep me on the go. We use all the wheat farmers can grow, and we keep a stable of eighty horses just to take the flour to the shipping ports."

"I know," Banneker said with a laugh. "The

flour from Ellicott's Mills is becoming famous around the world."

As George Ellicott turned to leave, he took a long look at the rough table on which he had placed his books. "You need a larger surface for your studies," he said, rubbing his chin thoughtfully. "We have a table that has been in our family for generations. I think it would suit your purpose perfectly."

Banneker watched his friend gallop away, then rushed to look at his treasures. First he examined the contents of the cases. He inspected the telescope, the instrument that would make distant objects, like the stars, appear nearer and larger. He looked at the lenses and ran his fingers tenderly over the long tube. Turning to the second case, he picked up each of the drafting instruments George had brought, wondering what each had to do with astronomy.

"I'll soon find out," he spoke aloud, and turned to the books. There were four of them, two written by James Ferguson, the noted Scottish astronomer. Another text, Mayer's *Tables*, seemed quite difficult. A fourth book, Leadbetter's *Lunar Tables*, contained complicated charts and tables.

"I'll master these by the time George returns," Banneker promised himself. He knew that a student of astronomy needed a knowledge of higher mathematics. At least he had a head start.

He opened Ferguson's *Introduction to Astronomy* and began to read. The style was simple, and interesting. The wooden clock ticked away the hours, but the reader never lifted his eyes from the pages. Forgotten were his field work, his afternoon chores. Only when dark shadows blurred the words did he put the book aside. Hurriedly, he milked his cows, fed the fowls and farm animals, and gathered the eggs. After that he ate some leftover food, not taking time to cook.

By that time, it had grown dark. Banneker rushed to get the telescope. Putting his eyes to the eyepiece, he trained the telescope on the stars. "Beautiful!" he cried out. "What a glorious sight!"

The wonders of the sky opened above him like a canopy of black silk, studded with dazzling star-jewels. On the Maryland hillside there were no artificial lights, no smoke or smog to blur the sky. In the clear, cool night thousands of stars could be easily observed.

That night was but the beginning. George Ellicott's books and astronomical instruments opened a new world of learning for Benjamin Banneker. He was almost sixty years old, an age when many men begin thinking of retiring. He remembered his grandmother's lesson, that life is an adventure in learning.

His friend George could never find time to come and teach him the use of the telescope, but he did remember the study table. Banneker placed it under a window, not far from the clock. The heavy oval table, made of fine pinewood, had dropleaves that reached to the floor on either side. This allowed Banneker to make the top surface larger or smaller to suit his work.

Always thoughtful of his friend, George also sent along a saucer-type candleholder that was made of tin. Banneker used it along with his own black iron candlestick to give a brighter light for his nighttime reading.

With the books, the telescope, and the work-table, the self-taught scientist began the serious study of astronomy. Nearly every night he could be seen leaving his cottage, a blanket or a heavy cloak in one hand, the telescope in the other. There on the silent hills he would stretch out on his back and study the sky.

The simple telescope magnified the stars, and hour after hour Banneker would track them. Each night he picked out a constellation, a brilliant group of stars, and studied the cluster in the sky. The following day he would pore over the astronomy textbooks to identify the star cluster and learn all he could about it.

Weeks turned into months. The sky patterns changed with the cycling seasons. Still Banneker stayed up nights, gazing at stars until the rooster crowed and sunrays tinged the sky. Only then would he limp to his house and fall upon his bed to sleep. By afternoon he would be back at the oval table, reading and making notes, drawing and making maps of sky patterns.

The amateur astronomer had no heart for farming anymore. He tried, but his scientific studies took up too much of his time. It was hard to hoe and plow when his thoughts stayed on the stars. The crops went unhoed and unharvested. The animals sometimes waited hours for food. Fruit trees remained untrimmed, and mischievous boys stole the ripening fruits from the orchard.

Neighboring farmers would peek into Banneker's cottage and see him asleep while the sun was high in the sky. "What has come over him?" farmers asked one another.

They grew more puzzled as months passed. "Has Banneker grown lazy?" they wondered. "Has he gone crazy? Some say he may be drinking too much wine these days."

The farm folk could not understand that astronomy had opened up the most exciting road to learning that Banneker had yet taken. After a year of study, he decided that he was far enough advanced to begin making astronomical predictions. Sure enough, in 1789, he worked out the difficult calculations for predicting a solar eclipse.

He knew then that he would have to make a decision about his farm. But what could he do? Once again, the Ellicott family came to his aid. "Let us buy the farm from you," they suggested. "You can stay on the land as long as you live."

The more Banneker thought about this suggestion, the more sensible it seemed. He talked it over with his sisters who lived nearby, and they agreed with the plan. Both of them owned enough land for themselves and their children.

So Banneker set aside a small tract to keep for himself, including the site of his cottage. After that he wrote out an agreement to give the Ellicotts title to the remaining acres in return for a lifelong annuity.

"I believe I shall live fifteen years, and consider my land worth £180," Banneker began the unique contract. "By receiving £12 a year for fifteen years, I shall in the contemplated time, receive its full value." He further agreed that should he die sooner, the Ellicotts were at liberty to take possession of the land.

"Only Benjamin Banneker would think of calculating the number of years he will live," George Ellicott teased. The Ellicotts agreed to pay the twelve pounds yearly no matter how long their neighbor lived. Twelve pounds in English currency came to about thirty-two American dollars at that time. This was considered a lot of money in the late 1700s, and it gave Banneker enough funds to buy items he needed for his studies.

What he very often needed were notebooks— and paper materials were very expensive. Like a true scientist, Banneker kept careful records of his observations, calculations, and experiments. Some of his notes were kept in a large book he called his Journal. Other records were written in a smaller notebook he called his Commonplace Book.

George Ellicott stopped by whenever he could to give help and encouragement. True to his plans, he built a large house at the Mills and married the pretty young woman named Elizabeth Brooke. In one of the gabled rooms of the two-story granite house, he set up an observatory. There he and Benjamin Banneker could study the minute details of the heavenly bodies.

One day, as they watched the stars, Banneker shared with his friend an idea he had pondered for a long time. He had once given a hint of the matter in a letter to George. "Farmers could benefit from the facts I am recording every day," he now said. "I have no doubt that I could compile an almanac."

"An excellent idea," George approved. "You are an ideal person to make an almanac. You have become a skilled astronomer and mathematician. You keep excellent records and scientific notes. Besides, you read a lot, so you will be able to include literary materials along with the needed information on weather, tides, and such."

Both men knew that the almanac was one of the most popular books in American homes, second only to the Bible. Farmers needed almanacs to let them know the best times for planting seeds. Fishermen, shipmasters, and travelers needed this guide, which forecasted weather, winds, and tides. Housewives needed almanacs to give them remedies for sickness, recipes for cooking, and assorted hints on general topics. Children as well as adults read the publication to enjoy the literary features included. "The poor man's encyclopedia" was the phrase commonly used to describe the almanac.

Would a printer publish a book created by a black man? There was one way to find out. Banneker set to work compiling information to be put in an almanac for 1791. He looked forward to the coming year with happy expectation.

10. Laying Out a Capital City

On a blustery afternoon, Benjamin Banneker rode down the hill to Ellicott's Lower Mills. He tied his horse to a hitching post in front of the store and hurried inside.

George Ellicott rushed to meet him, waving a letter in welcome. "Here it is," Ellicott called out, his eyes reflecting the excitement in his voice. "Major Ellicott writes that he will come in a few days to take you with him."

"It seems beyond belief," Banneker said in a voice equally animated. "This will be the greatest adventure of my life."

The two men moved to a small room that served as an office. Sitting near a stove that glowed because of the icy chill, they talked about the letter that had come from Major Andrew Ellicott. This was the same Andrew who as a boy had helped his father, Joseph Ellicott, design the four-faced clock. Andrew Ellicott had now become the most notable surveyor in the nation. Just the year before, he had surveyed the western boundary of the state of New York. The letter told of a far more dramatic assignment.

"Major Ellicott's experience will serve him

well," Banneker mused. "President Washington chose wisely in giving him the commission."

"George Washington made another wise choice in making you Andrew's assistant." George Ellicott rubbed his chin in a reflective mood. "This will be the first time in our nation's history that a man of your race has received a presidential appointment."

"I know." Banneker nodded in agreement. "I will try to do justice to this high honor."

"You will," George reassured him. "Remember, it was none other than Thomas Jefferson who urged the President to appoint you."

The voices of Banneker and George Ellicott quickened as they talked over the events that had led to the receipt of the letter. The surveying task was part of a new undertaking by the young United States. Until this time the Congress had temporarily been sitting in first one city, then another—eight cities in all. Now Congress decided that the nation should have a permanent capital city.

But where? Congress left the choice to the President. In 1790 George Washington selected a centrally located spot near the majestic Potomac River, between the states of Maryland and Virginia. Each state donated a parcel of land for the project.

This ten-mile-square federal district had to be

surveyed before the city could be built. In January, 1791, President Washington decreed that this survey should be made, and Andrew Ellicott was the logical choice.

Ellicott, in turn, needed an assistant with skills in both astronomy and mathematics. The President and Thomas Jefferson, who was then secretary of state, readily agreed that Benjamin Banneker should be appointed for this position.

The recalling of these events that February day ended with Banneker and George Ellicott shaking hands gravely. They knew that the task ahead was a difficult challenge. The results could affect the development and the destiny of the country. A dynamic capital city, Americans hoped, would unite the various sections of the country, resulting in a strong union.

Suddenly, a look of consternation crossed Banneker's face. "My almanac! I must complete calculations for my almanac."

"Your country comes first," George Ellicott said firmly. "Besides, I know that nothing is going to keep you from taking on this challenge."

So it was that Benjamin Banneker rode home and began preparing for his new adventure. Minta and Molly shared his pride in the assignment. Their oldest sister was now dead, but her son, John Henden, kept in touch with

Banneker. John Henden promised to keep an eye on the place while his uncle was away. Molly's son, Greenbury Morton, agreed to care for the animals and the orchard.

What should he take with him? Banneker pondered this problem as he packed. His sisters came to wash and iron his best linen shirts and handkerchiefs to perfection.

Elizabeth Brooke Ellicott, George's young bride, came to Banneker's cottage and helped him pick out the coats and trousers she felt would be suitable. "You will be meeting some of the most distinguished leaders in the nation," she told him. "We want you to be as handsome as any man among them."

Benjamin did look handsome when he joined Andrew Ellicott at the Mills a few days later. The two men made a stunning pair as they rode away on horseback. Ellicott, at thirty-eight, was dressed in heavy woolen clothes, a close-fitting vest, and a tricorn hat. Banneker, a few months from sixty, was dressed in a neat, plain suit of heavy broadcloth. A broad-brimmed hat covered his curly hair, now turning gray. Surveying instruments and luggage were strapped behind their saddles.

They took the turnpike for the forty-mile trip, making a stop along the way for food and a brief rest. By the time they reached Alexandria,

Virginia, they were soaked from the icy rain that had been falling steadily. They found lodging at a popular inn looking out on the busiest part of the town. Alexandria was then a thriving tobacco-shipping port.

The next morning, Banneker went out to explore the site of the new city. He rode through wooded areas, broken here and there by cleared spaces of cornfields and tobacco farms and a few isolated farmhouses and fruit orchards. Deep in thought, Banneker tramped up and down the hills. His imagination saw far beyond the bogs and rough hills, the woodland and wild marshes. "The spot is perfect for a magnificent city," he told Major Ellicott.

Losing no time, Banneker and Ellicott set to work in the rain and fog. They hired workmen to chop down trees and bushes. They bought packhorses, equipment, and supplies. They set up a temporary camp. The President wanted the survey completed in a hurry so that plans for building the city could be approved.

Banneker and Ellicott made a good team. Ellicott decided to supervise the workmen in the field, while Banneker made the astronomical observations and mathematical calculations they needed. Their measurements must be precise. Jefferson said in a letter to Ellicott that the lines "must run with all the accuracy of which your art is susceptible."

Since the measurement of angles plays an important part in surveying, the two men needed a knowledge of geometry, trigonometry, and practical astronomy. They had to make difficult computations in order to determine such things as latitude, time, longitude, and azimuths (angles measured in a clockwise direction from any meridian).

And these computations were based upon observations made of the sun, stars, and other celestial objects. In making these observations, the heavenly bodies are assumed to be situated on the surface of a huge imaginary "celestial sphere" whose center is at the center of the earth. So, the measurement of horizontal and vertical angles could be done in relation to celestial objects.

This required an observatory tent. Ellicott and Banneker placed the tent upon the highest point of a hill. A hole was left open at the top, through which the sky could be observed. Major Ellicott owned some of the finest surveying and astronomical instruments in the world, along with some of the most up-to-date reference books. Banneker made up his mind to master both instruments and books. The observatory tent became his world. He even slept there.

By the end of the first week, the weather cleared enough for Banneker to make his first observations. The powerful telescopic instruments magnified the stars in a manner he had never imagined. After a time, he was expertly recording the position and movement of stars, sun, and planets. To avoid errors, he repeated the charting again and again, then took an average of the results. It was tiring, tedious work, but Banneker loved every minute of it.

In his sky-watching, Banneker became fascinated by astronomical time-telling. Ellicott gave him the responsibility for caring for his precious astronomical clock. There were only a few of them in existence. The precision timepiece, set in a tall case, needed constant attention. Banneker kept it wound and checked it periodically against his observation of the sun so that the time would remain correct. An astronomical clock, in addition to having a dial for local time, has dials to record positions of the moon, stars, and planets, along with a variety of other astronomical data.

Night after night, Banneker worked while others slept. By the time the sun rose over the tent, Major Ellicott would arrive from nearby George Town, where he slept. Sometimes Banneker would go with him to do field surveying, but more often he stayed to work in

the tent. In late afternoon he got a chance to sleep, but even then workmen came into the tent to ask questions, or he had to get up to check the clock by the sun. He kept this heavy schedule, seven days a week, with no word of complaint.

By the end of February the surveying was well under way. In March the engineer-architect began his work of designing the city. President Washington appointed Major Pierre Charles L'Enfant for this task. L'Enfant had come to America from his native France as a volunteer to fight with the American colonies during the War for Independence. He adopted the United States as his home and began a career of designing buildings and medals. It was L'Enfant who designed the Order of the Purple Heart, the medal awarded to American soldiers wounded in combat.

In addition to L'Enfant, the President also appointed three men to serve as commissioners to supervise the city planning. The day came when Ellicott began meeting with these commissioners. He persuaded Banneker to go along.

When they entered the room for that first meeting, the faces of the commissioners registered their surprise. What?—their expressions asked—should a black man sit at discussions regarding the most important project in the nation?

It did not take long, however, for Banneker's quick mind and imaginative ideas to change their doubts to praise. After the first meeting, the men accepted him as a regular member of the planning team.

In late March, George Washington rode down from Philadelphia to examine the surveying. He spoke of his pleasure at the progress being made. The following month another dramatic event took place, one that touched Banneker deeply. He watched the colorful ceremonies that observed the laying of the first boundary stone.

The stone was placed at the point from which the surveyors ran the first line of the federal district. In the ancient and colorful Masonic rites, the stone marker was dedicated with grain, wine, and oil. The grain was used as a symbol of goodness and plenty, the wine as a symbol of joy, and the oil as a symbol of peace.

Goodness and plenty, joy and peace! Banneker echoed these hopes for the new city he was helping to build for a growing nation.

Another high moment came when Ellicott and Banneker determined the central point of the city. Working with their notes, they plotted a perfect line running due north and south. This line they crossed with another running east and west. On the hill where the two lines crossed, a hill covered with dense trees, they marked the center of the city.

Pierre L'Enfant looked at the hill and described it in a letter to Thomas Jefferson: "a pedestal waiting for a monument." On his plans he drew a fitting monument—the Congress House, or Capitol. On a second hill, covered by an orchard, he marked the site of the President's palace, later called the White House.

L'Enfant put his heart into the city planning. He studied plans of all the major cities of Europe and vowed to make the American capital the "City Beautiful." In a letter to the President, he reminded him of the unique venture. "No nation ever before had the opportunity offered them of deliberately deciding upon the spot where their Capital City should be fixed."

In his planning, the architect drew a grid of city blocks, with streets laid out in checkerboard fashion. The east-west streets were named alphabetically, and streets running north and south were named for numbers. Broad avenues, called by states' names, were planned to fan out from central points like spokes in a giant wheel. Most streets during these times were less than fifty feet across. L'Enfant planned for streets over one hundred feet wide and for one grand avenue four times wider. To add to the symmetrical beauty of the city, the architect planned public parks, fountains, circles, and monuments.

Benjamin Banneker thrilled to the idea of these grand plans. He liked L'Enfant, and whenever he got a chance to talk with him or to learn details of his plans, he made the most of the opportunity.

Unfortunately, the commissioners did not share this admiration. "Good land is being wasted to make wide avenues," they complained. "There are too many public parks."

"Make no little plans when building a capital," L'Enfant said in answer. "The city must be magnificent enough to grace a great nation."

The commissioners demanded maps of the plans so that lots could be sold. L'Enfant refused, knowing that land speculators would buy up choice spots.

The friction came to a crisis when the nephew of one of the commissioners began building a manor house on a spot that would block a major avenue.

"The streets and avenues must be laid out before houses go up helter-skelter," L'Enfant insisted.

The powerful landowner refused to move the structure. So L'Enfant sent a crew of workmen to dismantle the half-finished house and move the materials out of the way.

This was too much for the city commissioners. They complained to President Washington. At that time the President and Jefferson were busy with problems of running the country. The two sided with the commissioners. Reluctantly, the President notified L'Enfant that his services were at an end.

Deeply hurt and heartbroken, L'Enfant left, taking most of his completed plans with him. With his departure, Washington and Jefferson were left with a ten-mile square of muddy land and no plans for changing it into a city. If the project took too long, Congress might well withdraw support and not vote the funds they needed.

The two leaders turned to Andrew Ellicott for help. Could he finish the surveying and map the city as well?

Major Ellicott agreed and turned to his faithful assistant. "Will you help me?" he asked Benjamin Banneker.

"I will assist in every way I can," Banneker readily agreed. By this time he had returned to his home in Maryland and was hard at work on his almanac.

Once again Banneker put aside his own work to help plan the city. Working together, he and Ellicott were able to draw new plans, based upon their knowledge of the designs of Pierre

_ L'Enfant. Their task was not insurmountable because they could use notes from their actual survey of the ground. Fortunately for America, the plans were eventually completed.

In later years, many people have insisted that it was Banneker who saved the city by drawing L'Enfant's plans from memory. Some scholars believe that this story is only part fact and the rest legend.

The bulk of Banneker's notes, which might have given full details, were lost in a tragic fire. Many of Major Ellicott's papers were lost or stolen during another misunderstanding with the commissioners.

What is known beyond the shadow of a doubt is that Banneker assisted in laying out both the federal territory that became the District of Columbia and the capital called Washington City. As he had envisioned, Washington, D.C., developed into one of the most elegant and symmetrical capitals in the world. Visitors from all over the world find pleasure in its spacious, graceful charm. Benjamin Banneker, the self-taught astronomer, helped to create this historic loveliness.

11. Almanac Maker

Benjamin Banneker was happy to be home again during the summer of 1791. He had returned a hero. The inhabitants of the region hung on his every word as he described the exciting work being done to build the city of Washington. Sometimes these listeners stopped him as he walked or rode through the countryside. Many came to his cottage to talk.

That summer he raced to complete his almanac in time for publication. Almanacs usually appeared in October or November for the coming year. Banneker had no assistant, no secretary. The astronomer had to do all of his observations, calulations, record-keeping, and writing himself.

His records had to be consistent and accurate. So one day Banneker rode to Ellicott's store and made a purchase that took most of the money he had on hand. He bought a three-hundred-page notebook, a handsome folio measuring nine by fifteen inches. The paper was heavy and of the finest quality.

Banneker took the folio home and began lining up the pages with headings and columns.

He had been buying almanacs through the years and was thoroughly familiar with the general format. First he used a calendar and outlined the dates for each of the twelve months of the coming year. For each day he would have to foretell certain events that would take place in nature—sky, air, water, and land.

To some people, this might have seemed an impossible task, but not for Banneker. From childhood he had been a student of nature, and he knew how to read nature's signs. During his work with Major Ellicott he had learned much about techniques for making astronomical observations and calculations. He had also become familiar with more reference books dealing with astronomy. So Banneker approached his task with confidence.

In his new folio, which he called his Manuscript Journal, he filled in all of the holidays for each month, placing each beside the date on which it would fall. He included other significant days, such as the chief religious and saint's days, along with days of historical celebrations.

That was the easy part. Banneker had to make calculations for an *ephemeris,* a table showing the computed positions of a heavenly body for every day of a given period. This required weeks of studying the sky—by night and by day—and countless hours of mathematical computations.

Many almanac makers did not try to do this, but simply borrowed such tables from the works of other astronomers. For example, when Benjamin Franklin published his famous *Poor Richard's Almanac*, he used charts and tables made by others.

Banneker preferred to compute his own ephemeris. He did check his figures against available references, such as the *Nautical Almanac*, a reliable publication from England.

Some of Banneker's most difficult mathematical computations were done in order to predict the lunar and solar eclipses for the coming year. Since most people of these times lacked schooling in science, they could not imagine the reason for these glorious phenomena of nature. To many observers, an eclipse seemed an ominous or supernatural sign. They wanted to know the exact time when each would be visible over the area where they lived.

So Banneker had to establish the month, day, hour, and minute for each occurrence. He determined each lunar eclipse, when the earth would come between the moon and the sun, casting its shadow across the moon. Likewise, he set down the times for each solar eclipse, when the moon would pass in front of the sun and block all or parts of the sun's surface from view.

Rural farm families were awed by such a spectacular sight.

The calculations and diagrams needed to make these predictions took weeks of hard work and study. Luckily, Banneker had managed to do some of the work during whatever free moments he could snatch while working in Washington. For just one eclipse he had to make more than sixty mathematical calculations! Sometimes mistakes were made in his figuring, and he would painstakingly go over his calculations again and again until he found out where he had gone wrong.

Using similar methodical calculations, Banneker made charts and tables to show the rhythmic ebb and flow of the tides; the rising and setting of the sun, the moon, and bright stars; and other astronomical occurrences. One very useful table that Banneker compiled for his almanac was a tide table for Chesapeake Bay. This information would prove invaluable, he knew, to those navigators and fishermen who made a living along the bay and the rivers that emptied into it. No other almanac included such a table.

Weather forecasting made up another useful feature of Banneker's almanac. For years he had been keeping records of weather patterns. As an almanac maker he had to track the weather for the present, study the weather patterns of the past, and then forecast what the weather would likely be for the year ahead.

In this he trusted his keen senses. Early morning or afternoon often found him out on the hills, looking up into the expansive face of the sky, reading the signals being sent by clouds. He had learned to interpret the quantity, movement, shape, and height of clouds as clues to the coming weather.

Along with cloud signs, Banneker explored wind messages, charting such clues as speed, wind shifts, air temperature, and air currents. From his parents he had learned the everyday signs. Did smoke rise straight up? Was the wind gentle on his face? Were tree leaves fluttering or moving gently?

The farmer-scientist also learned to observe animal behavior for hints to seasonal weather changes. Did the squirrels begin gathering nuts earlier than usual? Were insects flying low to the ground? How many chirps did a cricket make in a minute?

Of course some of these signs were based upon legends, but these, too, played a part in weather forecasting in the eighteenth century. Scientists and inventors had not yet discovered the principles or invented the instruments needed for precise weather forecasting. Each almanac maker used his own system. Many depended upon astrological signs, believing that the positions of the moon and the planets determined the weather.

Through the years, Banneker had kept accounts of weather proverbs and legends and had also referred to these in his attempts to predict the weather. Some were fairly reliable; some were only fiction.

> When ants scurry into their hills and close the entrance, prepare for a rainy period ahead.

> A double rainbow signifies a long spell of dry weather.

> If bears hibernate early, it portends a hard winter.

> Early insects, early spring, good crops.

By analyzing weather signs and recording weather observations over a period of time, Banneker was able to establish fairly reliable weather predictions. For example, if both his records and the records in past almanacs showed heavy rains for the first week of April, he could safely predict a rainy spell for the same period during the coming year. If he could not find a predictable pattern, he then had to determine what atmospheric conditions might reasonably be expected.

The day finally came when Banneker had drawn all the diagrams and figured out all the charts and tables he needed for his almanac. He had completed all of the mind-boggling mathematical computations without benefit of adding machine, calculator, or any other timesaving devices available to modern mathematicians.

An almanac must entertain as well as instruct, Banneker reminded himself. For the entertainment features, he assembled an assortment of essays, poems, recipes, hints for curing ailments, and words of advice on many topics.

There was one last item. Readers would want to know when the various courts of law would be in session. Banneker located this information and wrote down the days for holding the Supreme and Circuit Courts of the United States—not only in Maryland, but in Pennsylvania, Delaware, and Virginia as well.

"The time has come to make the final step," Banneker spoke aloud in his cottage. Now he had to copy the mass of information into a manuscript form that a printer could use. One morning when the wooden clock struck six he was already at the oval table. The typewriter had not yet been invented, so the copying had to be done by hand. Benjamin Banneker dipped his quill pen in ink and began writing.

1792
First Month, JANUARY, hath 31 Days . . .

Using the fine penmanship Molly Banneker had taught him, the almanac maker formed the letters and figures slowly and carefully. He wrote most of the day, stopping every now and then to check references or verify his figures. He relaxed at noon and ate a light lunch of fruit and milk, then went right back to work.

When the clock struck again at six, he rose stiffly and began to fix his evening meal. He cut

two thick slices of home-cured ham and put them in a heavy iron skillet over the open fire. In a large bowl he mixed some cornmeal, and made a dozen corn dumplings, his favorite dish. One by one he dropped the dumplings into the skillet with the meat to simmer. In another pot he cooked some fresh beans from his garden. These made up his simple supper.

After eating, the writer took a leisurely walk through his orchard, which now nearly surrounded his house. His arms, legs, and shoulders were still stiff from sitting and writing all day. Nevertheless, he went back indoors, lit his two candles, and began writing again.

So ran the cycle of Banneker's days—writing, checking, reading, verifying. One afternoon he put down his pen and gave a soft cry of triumph. "Finished!" It reminded him of the night he had finally perfected the workings for his wooden clock.

The manuscript was ready for the printer. But which printer? Benjamin Banneker had yet to find out. He tried three separate Maryland printers. Each turned him down. Undaunted, he looked for a firm willing to publish the work of a black astronomer.

12. A Letter
to Thomas Jefferson

Banneker studied a list of all the printing firms in Maryland. The one printer who interested him most was William Goddard, a member of a distinguished New England family and a partner in the firm of Goddard and Angell. He was well known as the publisher of a Baltimore newspaper, the *Maryland Journal*.

Mr. Goddard might be just the person, Banneker decided. Through his research on printers, he learned that Goddard was a man of daring ideas. He had planned and initiated the first regular mail service in the colonies. After the Revolution, his mail services were enlarged into the United States Postal Service. Banneker also learned that the editor-publisher had put out almanacs at one time in the past. Perhaps he would be interested in trying a new one.

So it was that one morning Benjamin Banneker dressed in his best suit and rode his horse into Baltimore Town, soon to become a city. He found the busy port teeming with trade and commerce. After pausing to view the sights for a moment, he located the office of Goddard and Angell.

As he had hoped, Banneker liked William Goddard at first sight. From the warm greeting he received in return, he felt that the publisher was interested in him.

The two sat down to talk business. "Your work seems quite thorough," Goddard said, scanning the pages of the manuscript. "I have been thinking of publishing an almanac, especially since most of my competitors are doing so."

"You will note that I did the calculation for my own ephemeris," Banneker reminded him.

The editor tapped his desk, his eyes thoughtful. "There may be an advantage in publishing an almanac by a member of your race. Yes, I could very well be the first to do so."

After more discussion, William Goddard came to a decision. "I am prepared to pay you a small sum for the privilege of publishing your work. If it sells well, you will receive an additional payment."

"Your terms seem reasonable, Mr. Goddard." Banneker added another thought, his success giving him boldness. "I should tell you that I plan to submit my almanac to publishers in other cities." He knew that it was quite common for an almanac maker to sell the rights to the publication of his ephemeris to several firms. Each firm would then add whatever additional materials it thought best.

Goddard made no objections to this plan, and the two men parted as friends. Banneker rode home whistling the way he had when he ran down the path for his first day in school.

Assured of a Maryland publisher, Banneker next looked for one in another state. For this he needed contacts, so he went to talk the matter over with George Ellicott.

"My first choice is Philadelphia," Banneker told his best friend.

"A good choice," George Ellicott replied. "A reputable Philadelphia publisher could give your almanac wide circulation. My brothers and I have many friends and business associates in that city. They will help us."

"You always have the right solution for me," Banneker said, giving his friend a grateful look. "I think you will be proud of my efforts."

"The Ellicott family will take pride in whatever you accomplish," George answered him. "Make another copy of your manuscript, and I will see that it reaches Philadelphia and the right people."

Before Banneker could make the copy, he suddenly fell ill. The exausting work in Washington City, coupled with the long hours spent in completing his almanac, took a heavy toll on his aging body. For a few days he despaired that he might not live to see his almanac published by anyone. Ever faithful, his two sisters came and nursed him back to health.

As soon as he could leave his bed, Banneker copied the manuscript, and George Ellicott saw that it reached the attention of friends in Philadelphia. Through the influence of these friends, the manuscript was accepted by one of the city's best known printers—Joseph Crukshank.

Banneker learned that Crukshank, like the Ellicotts, was a Quaker. Equally interesting was that he was one of the founders of the Pennsylvania Abolition Society. Benjamin Franklin became its first president. The abolitionist societies, with their branches in several Northern states, were organized to help free black persons and to work for a legal abolition of the restitution of slavery.

The more Banneker learned about Joseph Crukshank, the more he admired him. It was Crukshank who had published the first American edition of the poems of Phillis Wheatley, who as a young girl had been sold on the slave auction block in Boston. She had been befriended by the kind Wheatley family of that city, taught to read, and then encouraged to develop her talent for writing verse. She became an internationally known poet.

These facts reminded Banneker of another event with which he was familiar. When George Washington was appointed commander in chief of the American army, Phillis Wheatley wrote a poem about him and sent it to the general, along with a letter telling of her admiration for his courage. Washington thanked her in a gracious note, complimenting her on her talents and inviting her to visit him. Phillis Wheatley did visit the American commander at Cambridge, where the future President and his staff entertained her royally.

All of these recollections set up a chain of thought in Banneker's mind. He was becoming more and more saddened that America had not yet ended the slave system. True, he was heartened by the fact that the antislavery movement was spreading. Still, he felt that the top national leaders should show more concern for the fate of slaves.

One day Banneker sat at his worktable, his head in his hands, wrestling with this problem. There was something he felt compelled to do. "Should I take the risk?" he asked himself. "Do I dare make such a bold move?"

With a deep sigh he lifted his head and reached for a sheet of his best paper. "I will," he answered his doubts. "The time has come for me to speak out boldly. Slavery must end."

Benjamin Banneker began to draft an appeal to one of the most influential statesmen in the world:

Maryland, Baltimore County,
Near Ellicott's Lower Mills
August 19th, 1791

To Thomas Jefferson, Secretary of State.
Sir, I am fully sensible of the greatness of that freedom which I take with you on the present occasion; a liberty which seemed to me scarcely allowable, when I reflected on that distinguished, and dignified station in which you stand; and the almost general prejudice and prepossession which is so prevalent in the world against those of my complexion.

Banneker's thoughts tumbled out on paper, almost faster than he could put them down. The letter was scholarly, written in the long sentences and flowery style used by writers of that day. As his quill pen scratched away, Banneker grew bolder in his appeal. He knew that if Jefferson could be persuaded to speak out against the injustices suffered by slaves, other Americans would listen. Jefferson had once written, and many white people also believed, that the black race seemed to be mentally inferior to other races.

A LETTER TO THOMAS JEFFERSON

In his letter, Banneker reminded Jefferson of the words the statesman had written into the Declaration of Independence—that every person should have a right to "life, liberty, and the pursuit of happiness."

Here, Sir, was a time in which your tender feelings for yourselves engaged you thus to declare; you were then impressed with proper ideas of the great valuation of liberty, and the free possession of those blessings to which you were entitled by nature; but Sir how pitiable is it to reflect, that although you were so fully convinced of the benevolence of the Father of mankind, and of his equal and impartial distribution of those rights and privileges which he had conferred upon them, that you should at the same time counteract his mercies, in detaining by fraud and violence so numerous a part of my brethren under groaning captivity and cruel oppression, that you should at the same time be found guilty of that most criminal act, which you professedly detested in others, with respect to yourselves.

Banneker added many more paragraphs of similarly strong statements in his long letter. He ended by asking the secretary of state to accept a copy of his almanac.

I chose to send it to you in manuscript previous thereto, that thereby you might not only have

113

an earlier inspection, but that you might also view it in my own handwriting.

And now Sir, I shall conclude and subscribe myself with the most profound respect,

> *Your most obedient humble servant,*
> *Benjamin Banneker.*

After mailing the letter, the astronomer waited in suspense. What would Jefferson do when he read it?

He did not have to wait long for the answer. As he opened the reply from the secretary of state, Banneker's hands shook with apprehension.

Philadelphia, Aug. 30, 1791

Sir, I thank you sincerely for your letter of the 19th instant and for the Almanac it contained. No body wishes more than I do to see such proofs as you exhibit, that nature has given to our black brethren talents equal to those of the other colours of men, and that the appearance of a want of them is owing merely to the degraded condition of their existence.

Banneker's eyes widened in surprise when he read the last part of Jefferson's letter.

I have taken the liberty of sending your Almanac to Monsieur de Condorcet, Secretary of the Academy of Sciences at Paris, and member of the Philanthropic society, because I considered it as a document to which your whole colour had a right for their justification against the doubts which have been entertained of them.

I am with great esteem, Sir, your most obedient, humble servant.

Thomas Jefferson.

The letter from the great statesman gave Banneker a high measure of satisfaction. He knew that de Condorcet was a noted scholar and humanitarian. By having the courage to write to Jefferson, the Maryland astronomer had brought his almanac—and the plight of his race—to the attention of European men of state.

13. Almanacs for America

Announcement of the official publication of Banneker's almanac appeared in the *Maryland Journal*. In the issue for December 21, 1791, William Goddard notified readers of its coming.

> BENJAMIN BANNEKER'S highly approved ALMANACK, for 1792, to be sold by the Printer's hereof, Wholesale and Retail.

The almanac was published with a long and impressive title: BENJAMIN BANNEKER'S PENNSYLVANIA, DELAWARE, MARYLAND, AND VIRGINIA ALMANAC AND EPHEMERIS FOR THE YEAR OF OUR LORD, 1792.

The publishers, Goddard and Angell, used an introduction that proved to be as provocative as the title.

> The Editors . . . feel themselves gratified in the opportunity of presenting to the public, through the medium of their press, what must be considered an extraordinary effort of genius—a COMPLETE AND ACCURATE EPHEMERIS for the year 1792, calculated by a sable descendant of Africa, who, by this specimen of ingenuity, evinces, to demon-

116

stration, that mental powers and endowments are not the exclusive excellence of white people, but that the rays of science may alike illumine the minds of men of every clime.

The editors asked readers to accept the work on its "intrinsic merit" and to "forget the long-established prejudice against the Blacks." The closing section of the introduction informed readers that the almanac included a letter from Mr. McHenry.

Mr. McHenry! This was none other than Dr. James McHenry, the famous Maryland Senator. He had served on the committee that had framed the Constitution of the United States, and later had been appointed secretary of war. Fort McHenry, birthplace of the "Star-Spangled Banner," is named in his honor.

James McHenry's letter included a biographical sketch of Banneker's life, stressing his years of self-study, and citing the almanac as proof that black persons were not intellectually inferior to whites, saying, "I consider this Negro as fresh proof that the powers of the mind are disconnected with the colour of the skin."

Benjamin Banneker's almanac brought him far more fame than either his clock or his work in laying out the Capital. He became known as the "Amazing Afro-American Astronomer." His almanacs gave proof to the world that black people, if given education and equal rights, could produce scholarly and artistic works equal to those of any other race.

The almanac did more. Copies reached Europe. English statesmen introduced the name of Benjamin Banneker into the records of Parliament. In America, and in Europe, abolitionists began to use Banneker's life and works as an argument against the enslavement of black people. This influenced more people to join the antislavery movement.

Banneker accepted the fame with his usual modesty. While others sang his praises, he was hard at work on his almanac for 1793. He approached the task with even more confidence than before. The first almanac had been produced, not only by Goddard and Angell in Baltimore and Joseph Crukshank of Philadelphia, but also by a printer in Alexandria, Virginia. Printers and readers alike had faith in future almanacs by the Maryland scientist.

The 1793 almanac came out containing a surprise for readers. There, for all the world to read, was the long letter from Banneker to Thomas Jefferson. As if that were not enough, it was followed by the secretary of state's courteous reply.

The letters caused very little resentment

among almanac readers. On the contrary, they served to increase the popularity of the almanac and of the astronomer. They also gave the abolitionists additional fuel for their fight against slavery.

Another interesting feature of the 1793 almanac was a daring peace proposal—"A Plan of a Peace Office for the United States." The proposal called for the establishment of a Peace Office, headed by a Secretary of Peace as a member of the President's cabinet. This secretary would have power to establish and maintain free schools in every city, town, and village, in addition to working for world peace.

The plan was written in seven sections. The seventh section suggested that a large room adjoining the federal hall be set aside for transacting the business of the Peace Department. Above the office door would be engraved symbols of peace—a lamb, a dove, and an olive branch. Along with these, the plan proposed, would be an inscription in letters of gold.

PEACE ON EARTH—GOOD WILL TO MAN.
AH! WHY SHOULD MEN FORGET
THAT THEY ARE BRETHREN?

The 1793 almanacs proved even more popular than those of the previous year. Again a Baltimore edition was published by Goddard and Angell, a Philadelphia edition by Joseph Crukshank, and one by a firm in Alexandria, Virginia. By the third year, printers in several states vied for the chance to publish the almanac by the black scientist. Banneker's almanacs were selling faster than any others being published.

He tried to include special features in each year's almanac to give the issue distinction. He was ahead of his time in many instances. For example, he used one issue of his almanac to caution readers about the dangers of smoking.

Almanac readers looked forward to the stories, poems, and essays as eagerly as they welcomed the scientific information. Banneker was equally at home with literature as with science. All during the year he saved favorite poems, stories, articles, and interesting bits gleaned from his wide reading. A large part of his earnings went into buying books and instruments to use in his work.

Some of the literary pieces in the almanacs were written by Banneker himself. Some were submitted by friends, especially those who were abolitionists. Still others were selected by the various printers.

Several of the poems and essays used in Banneker's almanacs illustrate his fascination

with the universe and his awe of its splendor. A
poem in his 1794 almanac is an example.

> View yon majestic concave of the sky!
> Contemplate well those glorious orbs on
>   high—
> There Constellations shine, and Comets
>   blaze;
> Each glitt'ring world the Godhead's pow'r
>   displays!

During these years, Benjamin Banneker made
friends with three men who helped to save the
city of Philadelphia during a grave emergency.
One was white, Dr. Benjamin Rush, who was
perhaps the most influential physician in the
United States. Among the signers of the Declaration of Independence, Dr. Rush was also a leader
in the abolitionist movement. He encouraged
the achievement of black people who were free
and worked tirelessly to free those who were still
slaves. It is believed that the peace plan published in Banneker's 1793 almanac was written at
least in part by Dr. Rush.

Banneker's other two Philadelphia friends
were black. Both were preachers who had once
been slaves but had bought their freedom. One
was Richard Allen, and the other, Absalom
Jones. The Reverend Mr. Allen became the
founder of the African Methodist Episcopal
Church.

An account of the tragedy, in which Banneker's three friends played key roles was given in a Philadelphia edition of his 1975 almanac. The calamity had occurred in 1793, when a fearful epidemic of yellow fever swept over Philadelphia. People died by the hundreds. Each day the carts of dead bodies clattered over the cobbled streets. Many of the doctors died, and those who were left could not care for all the sick. People began to panic, and those who were well were afraid to go near anyone who was ill. Nobody wanted to bury the dead, and this caused the epidemic to spread further.

At this point, the black people of the city received an unusual request. Would they come forward to nurse the sick and bury the dead?

They came forward, led by Richard Allen and Absalom Jones. The two men worked day and night with Dr. Rush, learning how to treat the sick so that they could train others. They organized groups of black volunteers to nurse the sick, comfort the dying, and bury the dead. Without their unselfish work, far more people would have died before the epidemic ended.

Issues of the 1795 almanac included something new that created quite a stir. For the first time, a picture of Banneker appeared on the cover of his almanac. The likeness was reproduced from a portrait and done in woodcut. It showed him as he looked in younger years. Almanac readers had a chance to study his handsome features—the broad forehead, pointed chin, dreamy eyes, and proud bearing. Until this time, many readers could only guess how Banneker looked.

By 1795, the almanacs were being published in as many as six different states. The following year, one of the Baltimore publishers wrote an unusual preface to that edition.

GENTLE READER,

To make an ALMANAC is not so easy a matter as some people think—like a well furnished table, it requires to have a variety of dishes to suit every palate, besides considerable skill in the cooking—Now, as it is impossible to suit all the dishes to every particular taste, we hope you will not be offended, should you find any not entirely to your liking, as we are certain there are a great many which will suit you to a hair. . . .

But there is one dish we invite you to partake of, and we are prouder of it than of all the rest put together; and to whom do you think we are indebted for this part of our entertainment? Why, to a *Black Man*— Strange! Is a *Black* capable of composing an Almanac? Indeed, it is no less strange than true.

In the last paragraph of the preface the editors nudged the reader with a gentle reminder.

> The labours of the justly celebrated Banneker will likewise furnish you with a very important lesson, courteous reader, which you will not find in any other Almanac, namely that the Maker of the Universe is no respecter of colours; that the colour of the skin is no ways connected with strength of mind or intellectual powers; that although the God of Nature has marked the face of the African with a darker shade than his brethren, he has given him a soul equally capable of refinement.

When Benjamin Banneker read such statements, he realized that his almanac was having far-reaching influence upon the thinking of many white Americans. Far beyond his dreams, in his own way he was helping to build the bridge from slavery to freedom for all black Americans.

14. A Gentleman of Peace and Learning

Banneker walked from Ellicott's Lower Mills, his arms heavy with purchases from the store and mail from the post office. The summer day was clear and breezy. At such times Banneker enjoyed a brisk walk from his home to the Mills and back.

Sunshine slanted through the window above the oval table where he placed his packages and sat down to read his letters. Two of the letters came from readers who wanted him to know how much they enjoyed reading his almanacs. Another letter included a mathematical puzzle the writer asked Banneker to solve. Still another came from a printer, inquiring about the possibility of publishing future almanacs.

Putting aside the letters to be answered later, Banneker turned to record his purchases in his Commonplace Book. His scientific mind was attuned to record-keeping, and he kept notes of events that took place in his day-to-day living as faithfully as he registered his scientific observations.

That day in 1796 Banneker listed the items purchased that morning, heading the page with the three yards of Irish linen he'd bought so that Molly could make him a new shirt and some handkerchiefs. Under this item, he recorded the purchase of one book, one inkstand, two pounds of candles, and one-half pound of gunpowder. He still managed to go hunting every now and then.

After making his notes, Banneker went outside and sat under a wide-spreading pear tree in the orchard he loved so well. Every year since childhood he had watched the apple, cherry, pear, and peach trees bud, blossom, and bear fruit with the turning of the seasonal clock. He could see that the branches were now heavy with fruit ripening in the summer sun.

This spot in the orchard was his favorite place for relaxing and thinking. In the middle of the orchard a clear spring flowed and glittered. A graceful willow tree, keeping guard as it had done for years, stood beside the spring. Banneker's wicker rocking chair squeaked as it moved slowly back and forth. Before he knew it, his head was nodding in a peaceful doze.

"Mr. Banneker?"

The soft voice awakened the sleeper. Standing in front of him were two lovely ladies. "My name is Susanna Mason," one of them introduced herself. She turned to her companion.

"You probably know my cousin, Cassandra Ellicott."

"I do indeed." Banneker gave his most courteous bow. "What a surprise it is to see you today!"

"I have been visiting at Ellicott's Mills for several weeks," Susanna Mason explained. "I did not want to leave without meeting you." She paused and looked at the fruit trees. "Your orchard is one of the best in this part of the state."

Banneker smiled. "You do me double honors, Mrs. Mason. I have planted new trees every year for over half a century. Just last fall I set out more than twenty-five young pear sprouts."

The astronomer had grown accustomed to having guests appear suddenly at his cottage. He invited the ladies inside, and the three were soon deep in conversation. Susanna Mason informed him, her eyes filling with tears, that two of her children had died during the yellow-fever epidemic. Cassandra Ellicott talked about the recent death of her husband, John Ellicott, of the Lower Mills.

Banneker proudly showed his guests the wooden clock and explained the papers, instruments, and drawings that covered most of the oval table. "You will please me if you accept a copy of my latest almanac," he told them.

"How kind and thoughtful," Susanna Mason said gently. "You are as wonderful as I thought you to be." She paused. "One day I am going to write about you. Would you be kind enough to keep in touch with me? Perhaps you will send me one of your mathematical puzzles."

"It will be my pleasure," Banneker said, taking a notebook from a high shelf. "Now I must add your names to my guest book."

He did. The names of Susanna Hopkins Mason and Cassandra Hopkins Ellicott were added to the long list of visitors who had come to Banneker's cottage.

Much of Banneker's time was taken up with

entertaining such guests. In the midst of compiling an almanac, he would often have to stop and talk with them, never seeming hurried or disturbed. Some of these visitors came out of curiosity, wanting to see the black man who had risen from tobacco farmer to world-famous astronomer. Some were mathematicians with complicated puzzles or problems to present. Still other guests came simply to talk with the genius who could do so many things, and do them so well.

Despite his fame, Banneker saw no reason to change his style of living. He never built a big house or bought fancy furnishings. He preferred

to use the earnings from his almanacs to buy new instruments, journals, paper, books, and other things he needed to carry on his scientific studies.

Benjamin Banneker and Susanna Mason did keep in touch through an exchange of letters. She kept her promise and wrote a long poem to honor him. The poem was printed in several newspapers.

In a letter written to Mrs. Mason in 1797, Banneker mentioned that he had been ill again. "I have a constant pain in my head," he wrote. He added a postscript: "The above is mean writing done with trembling hands."

Reluctantly, Banneker had to face the fact that his health was failing. The responsibility for compiling an almanac every year became too taxing. His almanac for 1797 was the last of his publications, but not the end of his studies. He still continued to make calculations for an ephemeris every year, recording the data in his Journal or his Commonplace Book.

"Each day of living is an adventure in learning." This was Benjamin Banneker's life-long philosophy, even after age and ill health slowed him down. He remained a *philomath*, a student of learning, especially of science.

He took time to record the beauty of the changing seasons—a rainbow, a sudden thunderstorm, a fresh falling of snow. With the same care, he made notes on the habits of insects and animals.

In the year 1800, the farms in the Patapsco Valley swarmed with locusts, eating everything in sight. Banneker began to study the problem. He recalled that he had first seen a plague of locusts in 1749, as a boy. By tracing the pattern of the appearance of these insects, he became one of the first scientists to determine that they come only once every seventeen years and remain a short time.

Banneker also made a study of bees. He had kept his interest in bees since the day his father set up the family's first hive in the orchard. Day after day, Banneker sat beside the beehives, observing the habits of the tiny creatures as they went about the business of making honey. Later, the amateur naturalist wrote a report on the habits of bees.

These were pleasant peaceful years for the philomath. He found relaxation in weeding his garden and in taking daily walks over the fields and hills. He found joy in his studies and in his music. During the evenings, neighboring farmers often saw him silhouetted against his log house, playing his flute or violin. Most of all, Banneker found peace in reading his Bible, which he never failed to study every day of his life.

The Ellicott family kept close watch over their friend and neighbor. They continued to pay the annuity for the land, even though Banneker lived far longer than he had calculated in making their agreement. They built a Friends meeting house at Lower Mills, and Banneker went there often to worship with the Ellicotts and their friends.

George Ellicott's daughter, Martha, was a young girl during these times. She became as fond of Banneker as her father had always been. In later years, she wrote the first book-length biography of the Maryland astronomer. One passage describes the way Banneker looked in the meeting house.

> He presented a most dignified aspect as he leaned in quiet contemplation on a long staff, which he always carried after passing his seventieth year. And he worshipped leaning on the top of his staff. His reverent deportment on these occasions added to the natural majesty of his appearance.

The aging astronomer recorded his calculations for 1804. After that, he could make only a few notations from time to time. Still he read, computed problems, and always, always studied the stars.

One of the few extravagant purchases Benjamin Banneker made in his life was a new and expensive pocket watch. Although his faithful wooden clock still worked, the scientist kept the more elegant timepiece on the oval table while he studied and made observations.

In Banneker's almanac for 1797, a poem was included entitled "Epitaph on a Watchmaker." The poem might well have been a description of his own life.

He had the art of disposing his *time*
So well,
That his hours glided away
In one continual round
Of pleasure and delight,
Till an unlucky *minute* put a period to
His existence.
He departed this life
Wound up
In hope, of being *taken in hand*
By his *Maker*,
And of being thoroughly *cleaned, repaired,*
And set a *going*
In the World to come.

15. There Lived a Man

"The sun is going down. The stars will soon come out."

"Yes, good friend, the day has come to a close. Sunset over the Patapsco is a picture I take with me wherever I go."

The old man and his younger friend sat on chairs beside the doorway of the log house. The old man, Benjamin Banneker, was black. His friend beside him, George Ellicott, was white. This was a part of the beautiful story at Bannaky Springs.

The two friends looked out over the sloping landscape. Trees and bushes were changing from summery green to paisley patterns of orange and red and yellow. Homes and farms dotted the land that had once been wilderness. It was eventide, and autumn, 1806.

"We have seen many changes come to our region," George Ellicott mused. "Each month, it seems, a new family arrives from Europe or from another part of our own country."

"Grandma Molly felt that this community would grow," Banneker recalled. "I will be seventy-five years old in a few weeks. It seems that Maryland, the nation, and I have grown up together."

"How right you are. Baltimore Town is now the great Baltimore City, a rich economic center . . ."

"And the United States grows larger and stronger with each passing year. President Thomas Jefferson practically doubled the size of the country when he purchased the Louisiana Territory."

"There is one change I have much hoped for." Banneker's voice dipped sad and low. "I long to see freedom given to all members of my race. Instead, laws are being passed to take away rights that free black people once enjoyed."

"There is hope," George Ellicott encouraged. "The men and women in the antislavery movement are fearless and determined. My family and I will surely do what we can."

"The Ellicotts have enriched my life and the life of this state," Banneker reminded his companion. "I predict that Ellicott's Mills, too, will soon become a city."

"And what about you, Benjamin Banneker? You have brought a unique fame to our community. Be proud."

The two friends sat recalling the past for another hour, then George Ellicott said goodnight. Banneker walked slowly into his house, using a stick to steady his steps. He lit a fire in the wide fireplace to keep out the chill of fall. Then he put candles in his two candleholders and sat at the oval gateleg table to read. When the wooden clock struck midnight, he closed his book and went to bed.

In those days, Banneker no longer tried to make notes on his readings and his daily activities. His hands trembled from the after-effects of several recent bouts with sickness. Even though he lacked the strength to walk or ride to Ellicott's store, he still took daily walks for short distances.

Several days after the visit with George Ellicott, Benjamin Banneker went for his usual daily walk. The morning was crisp and clear, with fluffs of clouds sailing overhead. Banneker walked slowly, for his legs were stiff and painful. As always, he carried a long stick to help him move. Yet, he held his stout body surprisingly erect.

"It's a fine day, sir." A neighboring farmer met him as he walked along a path.

"A perfect day," Banneker answered, with a friendly smile.

The two men stood in the bright sunlight, talking about the harvest season. Suddenly, Banneker gave a deep sigh. He leaned harder upon his staff. As he put his hand to his head, his body swayed—

The neighbor caught him before he fell.

Putting his arms around Banneker's shoulders, the farmer helped the astronomer back to his house. Past the tall Lombardy poplar they walked slowly, through the orchard with the willow tree and the stream still rippling in the sun.

Once inside, Banneker glanced weakly toward the oval table. It was still covered with books and instruments. He took a long look at the wooden clock, still ticking away the hours and minutes. Then he let the neighbor help him to bed.

The eyes of the stargazer, who had seen so far beyond the sights of ordinary men, slowly closed. They never opened again. His gentle heart was still. It was October 9, 1806, a Sunday.

Minta Black and Molly Morton knew what to do when they were summoned. Their brother, who always made plans in a methodical manner, had told them ahead of time. The grieving sisters carried out his wishes to the letter, and at once.

Molly's son, Greenbury Morton, drove a wagon to the cottage, and on it loaded the oval table, the stacks of books, and the scientific instruments. Some of these had been gifts from George Ellicott, and Banneker willed that they be returned to his friend. He also left to George Ellicott several other items he owned and treasured. These included his Manuscript Journal, his Commonplace Book, copies of his almanacs, and his correspondence with Thomas Jefferson. Banneker's other possessions were left to his sisters.

It was lucky for history that Minta and Molly acted so quickly. For on the following Tuesday, just as Banneker's body was being lowered into the grave, his house caught fire. The old log building burned like paper. Nothing was saved. Banneker's wonderful wooden clock, his furniture, clothing, and most of his records and precious papers were all lost in the blaze. His Bible was saved only because his sisters had taken it with them before the funeral.

Benjamin Banneker was buried on his farm, beneath two tulip trees atop a hill. His grave may have been marked at the time, but years later no marker could be found. Not even a stone called attention to the spot.

During the century that followed, Banneker's achievements went practically unheralded. Because he was black, historians wrote very little about him. His countrymen failed to dedicate a memorial of any kind to the astronomer, mathematician, inventor, naturalist, writer, and almanac maker. The man who helped to lay out the capital city of the United States did not have a street or a park named for him anywhere.

Never mind. True heroes are never completely forgotten. In 1836, Rachel Mason, the daughter of Susanna Mason, began a search to locate the exact spot of Banneker's home and grave. A century later, in 1954, the State Roads Commission of Maryland, in cooperation with the Maryland Historical Society, installed a marker at the site where Banneker's farm and grave are believed to be. This historic spot lies in the community called Oella, not far from the present Ellicott City. A new memorial marker was installed in later years.

In recent years, Banneker's achievements as an American man of science have been widely recognized. Scholars study his letters, almanacs, and journals to learn more about the social and scientific history of the times in which he lived. Some of these documents are found in large libraries and archives such as the Maryland Historical Society, the Library of Congress, and the New York Public Library. Other of these important documents are owned by descendents of the Ellicott family.

It is interesting that people who knew Benjamin Banneker in person felt assured that his greatness would be remembered. Susanna Mason knew it the day she first met the stargazer sitting under a wide-spreading pear tree in his orchard. In the seventy-two-line poem she wrote to honor him, she said:

> Some men who private walks pursue,
> Whom Fame ne'er ushered into view,
> May run their race and few observe,
> To right or left if they should swerve,
> Their blemishes would not appear
> Beyond their lives a single year.
> But thou, a man exalted high,
> Conspicuous in the world's keen eye,
> On record now thy name's enrolled,
> And future ages will be told,
> There lived a man called Banneker,
> An African astronomer.

For Further Reading

NOTE: Martha Ellicott Tyson's work *Banneker, the Afric-American Astronomer* deserves special mention, as it is the original biography on Banneker upon which most other biographies have been based. The book was published in 1884 by the Friends Book Association of Philadelphia. More accessible today, however, and the most complete biography of Banneker to date, is *The Life of Benjamin Banneker* by Silvio A. Bedini, cited below.

Bedini, Silvio A. *The Life of Benjamin Banneker.* New York: Charles Scribner's Sons, 1972.

Bennett, Lerone, Jr. *Pioneers in Protest*, pp. 12-26. Chicago: Johnson Publishing Co., 1968.

Brawley, Benjamin. *Negro Builders and Heroes*, pp. 25-29, 295. Chapel Hill: University of North Carolina Press, 1937.

Child, Maria L. *The Freedmen's Book*, pp. 14-23. New York: Arno Press; New York Times Co., 1968.

Clark, Margaret Goff. *Benjamin Banneker: Astronomer and Scientist.* Champaign, Ill.: Garrard Publishing Co., 1971.

Dobler, L., and Toppin, E. A. *Pioneers and Patriots: The Lives of Six Negroes of the Revolutionary Era*, pp. 51-76. Garden City, N.Y.: Doubleday & Co. 1965.

Emanuel, Myron. *Faces of Freedom*, pp. 37-64. New York: Scholastic Book Services; Firebird Books, 1971.

Graham, Shirley. *Your Most Humble Servant.* New York: Julian Messner, 1949.

BENJAMIN BANNEKER

Haber, Louis. *Black Pioneers of Science and Invention,* pp. 1-12. New York: Harcourt, Brace & World, 1970.

Harrison, Deloris. *The Bannekers of Bannaky Springs.* New York: Hawthorn Books, 1970.

Klein, Aaron E. *The Hidden Contributors: Black Scientists and Inventors in America,* pp. 3-30. Garden City, N.Y.: Doubleday & Co., 1971.

Lewis, Claude. *Benjamin Banneker, the Man Who Saved Washington.* New York: McGraw-Hill Book Co., 1970.

Rollins, Charlemae H. *They Showed the Way,* pp. 20-23. New York: Thomas Y. Crowell, 1964.